A Life of Blessings

Michael Harold Brown

Spirit Daily Publishing
www.spiritdaily.com
11 Walter Place
Palm Coast, Florida 32164

The publisher recognizes and accepts that the final authority regarding the apparitions in the Catholic Church rests with the Holy See of Rome, to whose judgment we willingly submit.

—*The Publisher*

A Life of Blessings by Michael Harold Brown

Copyright © 2012 Michael H. Brown

Published by Spirit Daily Publishing

For additional copies, write:
Spirit Daily Publishing
11 Walter Place
Palm Coast, Florida 32164

or contact: www.spiritdaily.com

ISBN 978-0-615-60557-9

Printed in the United States of America   First Edition

For my parents

SAINT JOSEPH
Pray for Us

MEMORARE OF SAINT JOSEPH

REMEMBER, O most illustrious Patriarch St. Joseph, on the testimony of St. Teresa, thy devoted client, never has it been heard that anyone who invoked thy protection or sought thy mediation has not obtained relief. In this confidence I come before thee, my loving protector, chaste spouse of Mary, foster-father of the Saviour of men and dispenser of the treasures of His Sacred Heart. Despise not my earnest prayer, but graciously hear and obtain my petition . . . (*Here mention your request.*)

Let us pray.

O GOD, Who by Thine ineffable Providence didst vouchsafe to choose St. Joseph to be the spouse of Thy most holy Mother, grant, we beseech Thee, that he whom we venerate as our protector on earth may be our intercessor in Heaven, Who livest and reignest forever and ever. Amen.

Nihil Obstat: Reverend Monsignor David D. Kagan, V.G., J.C.L.
Imprimatur: ✠ Most Reverend Thomas G. Doran, D.D., J.C.D.
                Bishop of Rockford
                Given at the Chancery this 9th of July A.D. 2002

To order, contact TAN Books. Toll Free: 1-800-437-5876. www.TANBooks.com.

Preface

May the Holy Spirit come upon you as you read this book! That's our most ardent wish for this collection and adaptation of "self-help" and "inspirational" commentaries from our website, *Spirit Daily* (www.spiritdaily.com).

Life is short and a challenge. But we can live it with joy and with blessings when we live it with an inner purity and closeness to the Lord.

1

No Matter How Trapped You Feel, There's Always an 'Exit'

As the dear Virgin Mary once said at a very famous apparition site, *"In prayer you shall perceive the greatest joy—and the way out of every situation that has no exit."*

Do you ever find yourself in circumstances that seem at a dead end? Is life as blessed and happy as it should be (as you will see, it should be joyful!). Have you ever painted yourself into a corner?

Those questions seem to be a good place to start in this book that addresses our lives and our blessings!

There's a fascinating painting that pertains to this and has been venerated at a church in Perlach, Germany, since 1700. It was painted by an unknown artist and inspired by a meditation made by Saint Irenaeus—who once said: "Eve, by her disobedience, tied the knot of disgrace for the human race; to the contrary, Mary, by her obedience, undid it."

There we have it. *Mary, Undoer of Knots.* Now that's a title for her! As a pamphlet about it explains, the image shows Mary with a crown of twelve stars and a fluttering blue mantle. Around her are angels. Beneath her feet is the serpent—the one who ensnares and entangles.

The point: when Mary is invoked—leading the way to Jesus—she untangles our knots and it is then the serpent who is in a tangle (whatever the novena)!

As is also readily observed, one of the angels in the painting holds the ribbon of your life as the Blessed Mother calmly and easily goes about straightening out all the knots in it.

A mysterious and beautiful image this is! Usually we think of the knots in our lives as specifically troubling situations, but the "knots" are also problems we have had for years, anger, resentment, perhaps deep hurts between husband and wife, the absence of peace and joy at home, sinful inclinations. A knot can be a son addicted to drugs. It can be alcoholism. It can be guilt. It can be fear or depression or unemployment. It can be cancer. This, apparently, is where Mary Undoer (or "untier") of Knots comes in.

We also go to the angels. For the most part, we forget about them. And yet they stand ready to assist and eagerly anticipate it. There is Michael. There is Gabriel. When Raphael is involved, there can be healing (as well as with any others)! Most of all, we go directly to Jesus—speaking to Him through the heart more than the mind. Mary assists in this also.

Again we hear an echo of the words: *"In prayer you shall perceive the greatest joy and the way out of every situation that has no exit."*

Think of it: even when intellectually we can't figure out a resolution or means of escape, God can turn things around in such a way that there is a sudden opening; there are angels; we are suddenly saved.

Is the novena infallible, as claimed? Well, perfect faith—prayer with perfect faith—is infallible. That much we can say!

It's the key to blessings. Freedom comes for those who seek it. To be blessed is to be close to God. Holiness is the wisdom of His Power. There is always a way out. There is always a way to be blessed. It may be an exit to the eternal—death—true enough; it may not be how we would design it; but very often, practical earthly problems are solved when we simply remember to pray with humility.

Your life should and can be blessed (as we will see) at every turn!

2

Nothing is Impossible With Angels and God

There are many blessings of the Spirit, and God almost always has something surprising in store for *you*. When it comes to "gifts," what you need to do is pray for them.

We forget the simple admonition: ask and you will receive.

This pertains to gifts of the Holy Spirit. Incredible as it may seem, the miraculous is often there for the asking. We just don't ask! God flows through us when we go to Him as children with requests.

Although it's up to the Lord as to how He will answer, often He will grant the gift of tongues or prophecy or even healing to those who earnestly and diligently and faithfully request it. Prayers open the doors to grace that flows in powerful new ways, especially during Communion. *This is when the gates of Heaven open the widest* and it's the time for our most direct requests. And so during Mass, request spiritual gifts. Request the gifts of peace, joy, love, tears, wisdom, consolation, visions, happiness, discernment, knowledge, deliverance, understanding, love. Ask the Lord to have it so that angels surround you. Ask that you have a closer kinship with your angels. Ask for the gift of prayer so you always know what to pray for!

Make your requests and then watch—over time (God's time)—as they begin to manifest. Many gifts we never think to request. A beautiful gift of the Spirit is the grace to bring joy to all who are in our presence. We are all temples of the Holy Spirit and can pray that He comes in such a way that people feel joy when they're around us. What a gift that is! Pray for the Love of God to enter you (inhale it) and then exhale it to others.

As you do, you will not only bless (and heal) others but also yourself.

Pray to be a fount of the Holy Spirit. Pray to be His citadel. Pray to be a sanctuary. Pray for the whole range of gifts; the Lord will grant what fits your mission; once you feel a gift arrive, work at keeping it.

Nurture it. Watch it grow. Treat it preciously. Too often the Holy Spirit bequeaths something to us but then we begin to stray back into sin or worldliness. The gift diminishes.

On the other hand, when we're faithful, God "gifts" us freely. He sends us understanding and patience and long-suffering. He grants us the gift of mercy. Or charity. He may allow us to heal. He may allow us to glimpse the heavenlies!

Love. Patience. Healing.

Remember when Jesus told His followers to go to the sea, take up the first fish they caught, and look for a coin (*Matthew* 17:27)? It was a sign that He had orchestrated as He also orchestrates them for us. The more we meditate on what God already has done for us, the more signs He sends.

Remember in prayer to savor past times God has helped you. Love Him repeatedly for it. Recall every detail. Give thanks all over again (with the same specificity as the request)!

And with faith, keep the cycle going. Make your life a flow of miracles. *Jesus I trust in You. Jesus I trust in You.* The miraculous is there for the asking. There are exceptions. There are those trials of life. But God loves to operate in the realm of luck.

If, in prayer, you think back over your life, you'll suddenly find a steady stream of "lucky" incidents that changed your life. That's where we see God working many of His miracles. As one sage suggested, coincidence is God's way of remaining anonymous, and the dictionary tells us that coincidence is "a sequence of events that although accidental seems to have been planned or arranged" (which is correct, of course, about the events being "arranged," but wrong about them being "accidental").

I was saying a Rosary while waiting on a bus once during a trip to Africa, and as soon as I got back to my room realized that the beads—which I prized, because they seem to have turned gold—weren't around. They were lost. I thought I had put them on an empty seat next to me. But they were lost. I had misplaced them.

I searched everywhere in my room and several times: my shirt, my pants, my desk, my bed, under the bed, under the blankets, my computer case. When I heard the bus return shortly after, I dashed down, told the bus driver what had happened, and we scoured the vehicle—to no avail.

The beads were nowhere to be found. The next day, I alerted others on the pilgrimage and searched the bus a second time. They simply were not there. This was while visiting the apparition site of Kibeho in Rwanda. I returned home and as I was unpacking I reached into a pouch in my large, check-in bag and found the beads there! I *know* I didn't put the beads there. I never put them in any luggage. To my recollection, I had not even gone near the luggage, and they could not have fallen out of clothing into a tight pouch.

So I had recovered the Rosary but unpacking another bag, which I had placed on my bed, I realized, now, that a new pair of sandals was missing!

These I had kept in two pockets in the largest suitcase I had taken, and *only* in those two pockets. But now they simply weren't there.

I was distressed because they were unique sandals and I had purchased them just before the trip. I had only worn them a few times—in a pilgrim room, then a hotel near the airport—and now I had lost them. I was pretty sure I had packed them but there was a chance I had left them in the hotel (which was in Kigali, the capital of Rwanda). Now, at home, I searched through my luggage three or four times. I also searched my bedroom. Even though I had opened my luggage in that room, and nowhere else, I extended the search to the entire house and even outside the house. My family helped me. No "original Arizona Jean Company size-nine Brazilian-made sandals."

I thought of contacting the hotel but knew it would cost more to ship them than simply trying to buy another pair, which I resolved to do. Before putting it out of my mind, I asked for the assistance of the Blessed Mother and my guardian angel. While Africa is far away, I knew that time and space mean nothing to angels and they could get them back to me if God so willed.

After that heartfelt prayer, I did put it out of my mind; I wrote the sandals off.

A week later—late Christmas morning—I was walking across our house when suddenly smack in the middle of the family-room-dining-room vestibule, in one of the spots most readily visible and trafficked in our home (a place where nothing could go unnoticed), I spotted a pair of sandals and

realized to my shock that they were my prized lost ones—
the pair I had taken to Rwanda.

How possibly could they now be there right in plain
view? How did they get home? Was there someway my son
had worn them and left them there? He said no. My wife had
vacuumed that spot just minutes before. They had not been
there the entire week, that was for certain.

But there they were, late Christmas morning—the great
day of blessings.

3

Lost and Found

God is so good: He gives us little miracles; He gives us big ones. They're all a sign of His watchfulness (and that of angels).

Let's stay on the matter of lost items for a moment. After I ran an article on my lost rosaries, we received mail from others with similar experiences.

"I read the account about the rosary and have a very similar story," said one.

"In 1968, I purchased a rosary for my mom with one decade spelling her name—Theresa Ann. She attended Mass and accidentally left it in church. After many frantic calls: no rosary . . .

"My mom died in 1998 and two years later—in 2000— a nun at our parish stopped me to thank me for the box of rosaries left on her desk. (I make rosaries and have made over 24,000 for missions and priests.) She asked if I were positive that I wanted to give her the one rosary—and guess what? It was the rosary I purchased in 1968. I have no idea how it arrived at her office as I did not leave any rosaries for her!"

"Same thing happened to us about ten years ago when we were living in the northwest," added Peg Diesburg in Denver. "My husband misplaced his wedding band and we looked everywhere. Two weeks later it just appeared on our bedroom dresser after coming home from Mass—and after giving up on ever finding it again. We still talk about it appearing out of nowhere and that it had to be a miracle."

"I loved reading your story about the miraculously returned sandals," said Jane Griffin in St. Louis, Missouri. "I, too, had a similar experience last year.

"In July a dearly loved cousin, who was a very devout nun, passed away. Two days after her funeral my husband realized he could not find some very important documents he needed for a report he was working on. We searched *everywhere* and had about given up—when I recalled having read a few times that sometimes our Lord will allow the recently deceased to do favors as a consolation to their loved ones still on earth. So: we prayed and asked if Sister Jean would please help us find the papers. A short time later my husband called me to come in to the dining room.

"There—on an *otherwise* empty dining room table, one we had seen countless times—were the papers neatly stacked. A miracle for sure!"

Try hard enough, and you can raise questions. There are always possible "explanations." Absent-mindedness? Jet lag? We can only imagine how the Blessed Mother and St. Joseph felt after losing and then finding Jesus!

"About your rosary beads," wrote Dr. Thomas F. Warner, professor of surgical pathology at the University of Wisconsin: "I was on my way to a pilgrimage site several years ago and lost my rosary ring at O'Hare Airport. I looked everywhere, especially since it was from Medjugorje. I was upset. I arrived in Boston for the trans-Atlantic connection and when I got up from the plastic seat in the waiting lounge, there it was on the seat."

That reminds us of an account from the west coast of Florida where a woman lost her watch in the Gulf of Mexico and then spotted it subsequently while she was fishing miles away!

Added Julie Stumphauzer in Vermilion, Ohio: "I just read your article on the lost rosary and sandals you had restored to you, and I could relate to it.

"Just a few weeks ago, I too had such an experience.

"In October, we had taken our son to Philadelphia to deploy for Africa in the Peace Corps. After two other overnight stops, we arrived back home. Upon unpacking, I discovered that I had lost one of the diamond stud earrings that my husband had given me years before!

"We searched everywhere—both in the luggage and in my jewelry armoire until I finally resigned myself to the loss. Near the end of November, I took the remaining stud to a local jeweler to see what a duplicate would cost. They had the piece for a few days.

"Then one morning the lady there called me to give me the price quote—$500, which was far too expensive for our budget. I thanked her but declined, and said I'd be in to pick up the single stud that day. I hung up the phone, said a quick prayer like, 'Well, Lord, I guess I'll just have to do without them from now on'—then suddenly remembered something: that very morning I had opened the tray of my jewelry box, seen the single stud lying there, and thought to myself, 'Gee, it's too bad that the other is lost; what will I do with just the one?'—forgetting momentarily that I had already taken the other to the store!

"I slowly went back upstairs, opened my jewelry box, and in the top tray—in a place I had searched many times before, in plain sight, and which I used for other pieces every day and could not possibly have missed the earring sitting there—there it was.

"The lady at the store later was almost as elated as I was! I've never had this kind of gift from God before, but I truly believe He gave me a tangible sign of His Presence in my life at a time when I need to remember that He's always with me."

4

The Trials of Job?

This is victory—in Christ. Are you a victor or a victim? I heard a preacher ask this one night. It's a good question. We need to make sure the answer, of course, is "victor." That's the easy part. *But how do we "win"*—find happiness and miracles and blessings—in life?

The answer is with Jesus and how we view situations. First, take a look at your hearts. Be honest: Do you look at things positively or negatively? Are you looking to the future or mired in the past?

When we're living the past, we are often living through the lens of the negative—dwelling on past losses, pain, and injuries, which may mean we have bitterness in our hearts. In a way, our emotions, our hearts and souls, have been *marinating* in whatever it is that made us bitter. And when we wallow in it, we're losers before the game even begins.

Who hasn't done that? Who hasn't felt sorry for himself or herself? And sometimes, we have what seems like a darned good reason! There are folks who have suffered calamity after calamity—heartbreaks, accidents, cancer, and other serious disease, all in one horrid package. I have a friend who had this occur in the course of a few short years—along with family problems, loneliness, and struggles in the workplace.

Her response? At first anger at God. But she was courageous enough to shed this anger and it led to her conversion!

That's the result of making a decision for the positive *in all things*. It is to take a positive perspective. Yes, we know that we go through trials; yes, we realize the negativity; and, yes, we must be aware of evil. From time to time, the enemy attacks.

But we are called to transcend. And we do that by making the simple decision to accentuate what is positive.

We can take all past sorrows and hurts and give them to Jesus in the Blessed Sacrament.

Take them to Him and watch darkness vanish.

Look at the *Blessed* Mother. Most women who became pregnant before marriage, saw the scorn that would come with it, couldn't find a place to give birth when the time came, then were chased down by a brutal tyrant, lived in the poorest of circumstances, and later watched there sons murdered in the most brutal fashion would be pretty bitter! But Mary was not—and all generations have seen her as blessed ever since! "Defeat" became victory.

Talking positively, thinking positively, and acting positively—seeing His Light at the end of the tunnel—draws the positive like a magnet. Watch that happen to you. Expect good to come (really *expect* it) and watch in God's time how it alters your reality.

Hope leads to trust which leads to the miraculous.

On the other hand, when we're negative we draw things that will be (increasingly) bad. We especially attract such negativity when we dwell on past hurts. Too often we immerse ourselves in self-pity.

This is where the enemy hooks into us. This is where he causes real damage!

Through Christ, *we*, not the past, should take control of what happens to us. Did Jesus not come to grant us that victory and life more abundantly (*John* 10:10)? You have to tap into that.

We may not be able to undo negativity in our pasts, but we have a *lot* to say about the future—and a positive future means a positive attitude.

For this we often need forgiveness. Did you ever notice how repeating a negativity—*dwelling on it*—magnifies a painful memory?

With Christ we leave past hurts in the dust of a positive outlook that speeds us from painful thoughts.

Bitterness is an acid, the bitter marinade, that eats at us and is morbid.

Simply, do not allow yourself to get depressed. Clinical, you say? A psychological issue?

Perhaps, in certain cases. But too often depression is a spiritual issue—one we can control by moving on, praying, and making the decision to let our wounds heal.

Dwelling on past hurts is like picking on a scab—which not only inhibits healing but leaves scar tissue.

Make a decision not to be sad. Make a decision not to be mad. Make a decision to forget the wound and let God heal it.

The "trials of Job"?

When met by faith they always turn into the greatest periods of grace.

5

A Beggar and Turkey Bacon

God works when we tough it out, maintain goodness, and keep our eyes spiritual. A great example of this comes to us from Jo-ellen Ridley of San Diego.

"I would like to share this amazing experience I had, so that others may know that God is really there," she said. "Last year I was experiencing some difficult times in my life. My husband's employer went bankrupt and he lost his job at age fifty. In addition, we discovered that his boss had stolen $8,000.00 of our retirement money. My son decided to move back home to help us pay the bills, but within three months he lost his job as well. The financial stress was very great and my husband started having severe panic attacks and needed medication to help him cope.

"I have a part time job which does not pay very much money, but I was praying all the time and trying to stay positive for all our sakes. As part of my job, I would drive to the post office every day to drop off the company's mail.

"Every day at the intersection where I needed to turn was a bum holding a sign asking for help. I felt sorry for this man and would talk to him. His name was Alan and he was dirty and had only a few teeth. I would give him a dollar or two every time I saw him. I knew he had it worse than we did. There was a day I had no cash to give him and he told me that it was okay he just appreciated having someone to talk to.

"I was on my way into work one morning and was feeling very overwhelmed by all the things I needed to do (I had to put my house up for sale and start packing). I said a little prayer to God and asked Him if He could help me remember to buy some turkey bacon on the way home, so that I could make it for dinner. I'd forgotten to buy it the day before and it was just one more of the things on my list to get done.

"I made my usual trip to the post office and saw Alan again begging at the light. I rolled my window down to give him a dollar, when he suddenly reached down into his bag and said 'I have something for you if you would like it.'

"He handed me a package of cold turkey bacon and asked if I could use it.

"He explained that a few minutes earlier a women had given him a bag of groceries, and that since he was a bum he had no way to cook it. I was stunned and said thank you very much I sure could use it. I drove off thinking did that really just happen? A bum gave me the turkey bacon I needed? I was absolutely floored! I realized that it was God's blessing for me to let me know that He hears me. I felt a wonderful sense of peace come over me and I knew everything would be all right. It took some time and a lot of faith to get through this period, but I knew because of the turkey bacon that God had a plan. One year later we moved into a bigger, nicer home in a new neighborhood. My husband got a wonderful new job with great benefits and my son finally got a new job as well! Any time I start to feel down about something I just think of turkey bacon and feel a whole lot better. I felt it was important to share my story with you, so that other's can hear of this little miracle in my life, and know that God is always there for them."

6

Heart Communication

If you want to be blessed, first be a blessing to others. That was another sermon I heard. Too often, we become ensnared in our own little world. We become entangled in *our* problems. We're always looking inwardly and we're always getting stalled on some issue that then hovers like a crisis.

Yet, the more we dwell on a problem—the more we pity ourselves, instead of exercising faith—the more entrenched those problems become.

When we get depressed, it's often because we are thinking only of our own dilemmas, which is unfortunate because God wants us to keep our eyes not on ourselves but on the needs of others.

Look at Jesus. His entire life was spent blessing others. Despite His inconceivable suffering on the Cross, He was looking out for folks other than Himself: the thief who was crucified next to Him; His mother, standing there next to John; and every one of *us*.

We're called to do the same. We're meant to *give*. God wants us to be the vessels of His mercy. That means lifting up *others*. Try spending your time thinking of the problems *others* face and you'll see how your own troubles lessen.

Help others and God will solve *your* problems. When you feel sad or depressed, take your eyes off your own situation and set them on those around you.

Notice the needs of people God has set in your path.

Pray about ways of solving someone else's problems.

Pray to be a source of constant *encouragement*.

The next time you feel like criticizing someone, stop. Hold off. Put it aside.

Keeping our mouths shut opens the Kingdom of heaven.

God loves silence. He loves when we contemplate. He loves when we suffer quietness instead of mouthing off (unless correction is truly warranted).

You'll feel filled. Prayer will come easier; when you don't criticize, you're closer to God.

Of course, this is easier said than done. Criticizing others is a natural proclivity. It's a manifestation of pride. We do it to try to elevate ourselves. It's also a manifestation of envy. Putting down someone else makes us feel superior. But the feeling is temporary and stops blessings.

You'll note that the Pope rarely if ever criticizes a person by name. The same was true of Jesus. It was the matter of casting the first stone, and yet we live in a society that is obsessed with doing just that. Our television and radio shows are full of broadcasters whose claim to fame is downing others—and when we listen, when we enjoy someone besmirching another, when we enjoy a constant spewing of negativity—we become participants. There is a loss of grace. It comes back to bite us.

Next time you feel like pointing out the negative in someone, first try to be that person's "defense attorney." Remember, prosecution can be persecution. Try helping them. Imagine their circumstances. Strive to see the good parts of a personality, and focus on those. Ask yourself if you have ever done something similar. See all the reasons a person may have done what she or he did. That's what God does, and thank God for that!

There is good in every darkness, and there are countless ways we're given the chance to help. How do we do this? We lift others up. We compliment them. We let them know we love them. As a prominent preacher said, it's not enough to simply feel love. We have to show it. We have to express it. Love is not love, in a sense, until we give it away—and we should be doing so at every opportunity. Help someone else and God will help you. Pray for those who despise you, and you will not feel their sting. Come to the aid of another, and God will come to *your* aid. Instead of your problems, instead of what *you* need, focus on being a blessing.

Aim on fulfilling what someone else needs.

This is the most powerful way of drawing down God's grace, and you'll be astonished at the result. God has created all of us to serve each other. He wants *us* to be blessings. And when we begin looking at life that way—when we become unselfish and see the opportunity to do good in every circumstance in life—the Lord blesses us without our even asking for it.

Meanwhile, we must pray from the heart.

It's those "heart prayers" that count the most. Direct communication.

The heart is a transmitter. It is also a receiver. Somehow, it has strong spiritual links. Some say it's the home of the spirit.

Soften up. Harden not (*Psalms* 95:8). Every once in a while, have a good *cry*. You heard me right: weeping is a gift from God (when it's not morbid); it empties us; it releases emotions that can eat away (like acid); it has a cleansing effect. When we cry, the heart is engaged (whereas a dry eye can indicate a parched heart).

Christ wept. So did those who sought (and won) His cures (for example, the blind man: *Mark* 10:47-51). He responds to cries because He responds to words *from the heart*. We're told that John Paul II prayed with a wailing that at times was heard outside of his chambers. There is even a charism know as the "gift of tears." My wife has this. Whenever she comes across something that's anointed—something that's especially powerful—tears fill her eyes and she can't stop them.

That's the Holy Spirit at work—purging, touching. We are healed by the *tears of miraculous statues*. One man we know who has this gift says he knows regular crying from spiritual crying because when the gift of tears comes, his nose doesn't run!

For the longest time, I had trouble crying. I couldn't do it even when I tried to force myself to. Then, in 1995, during a trip to France, I visited the tomb of St. Therese the Little Flower, and as I approached it I suddenly found myself in a flood of my own tears. In an instant, emotions were released that had been pent up for years. I have cried since then and am happy about that. As one preacher noted, if you look at the Son of God without tears to protect your spiritual eyes, you'll go blind. The greatest reapers, he said, are the greatest weepers!

With our tears, Heaven touches. God saves them up. Did you know that? The tears we weep are gathered. "My wanderings you have counted," says *Psalms* 56:9, "my tears are stored in your flask."

I have actually spoken with people who had the near-death experience and testified that all their tears had been kept by the angels like jewels on the other side of the veil.

With God, nothing is wasted, no emotion is unnoticed, and no cry—when righteous—is passed. As kids depend on adults, so must we depend on Him. Did not Jeremiah cry out for his eyes to be a "fountain" of tears?

"I have heard thy prayer," says *II Kings* 20. "I have seen thy tears." We suffer because we are joint heirs with Christ. Did He not cry out to the Father?

In weeping, our souls, our needs, our anxieties are poured forth. "They that sow in tears shall reap in joy," the Bible (*Psalms* 126:5) promises us. The Lord wants our emotions engaged. He wants us to put our hearts into *everything*. Our hearts are more important than our minds. Let us remember how valuable—how precious—it was when that sinful woman used her tears to wash the Lord's feet (*Luke* 7:38)! Remember that feeling is more important than reason. Not that we shouldn't think. We just need to remember that what we feel in the deepest part of our souls is what God hears most audibly and that the greatest distance on earth can be between the head—the brain—and the heart (chest).

"I have seen thy tears," says 2 Kings 20:5. "Behold, I will heal thee."

7

Those Who Love God Have a Glow of Well-being

So now and then, go ahead. Cry up to God. Let Him know where you're at. Let Him know what you need. Show Him your tears—and watch how powerfully He responds. God designed the world so that our greatest joy is closeness to Him.

No matter what you seek in life, no matter how much money you have, no matter your luxury, you'll never get greater pleasure than simply lifting your heart to the Lord.

Meditate on that: the basic act of worship is the source of highest gladness. And it's free! When we seek God—when we love Him, when we *adore* Him—He draws us above all physical circumstances.

No matter what you may be going through (pain, depression, worries), if you praise God, He will bring you to joy.

Praise brings us close to Him and there is no joy like the joy of knowing the Lord. He sends graces that can defy our circumstances. He brings joy where, by the standards of the world, there should be depression. He brings happiness where there is frustration. He delivers joy where there is discouragement. There are those in poverty. There are those who are lonely. There are those with cancer: In God they find what they need.

The opposite is true of those who ignore God and thus set themselves at a distance from Him. Take a look around and you'll see many "rich" people with grim looks. No matter what they accomplish on earth, they never find true gladness because they don't have a closeness to God.

Meanwhile those who love God have the glow of well-being.

To draw close we must love Him and seek to do His will, to be what he planned for us to be. We must seek Him in everything. Then comes a bliss that's indescribable. You can buy a yacht or a Mercedes—you can marry well, you can be the most powerful person on earth—but if you don't have God you have not experienced true happiness.

You have missed out on that transcendental elation— that ineffable joy that put a smile on the faces of so many saints who to the world seemed poverty-stricken.

Remember that smile on the face of Mother Teresa?

When we pray, God grants us feelings that can not be attained elsewhere. God is joy. It's that simple. There's nothing you can do that will bring as much contentment. Adore God through the day. Do it from the heart. Love Him. Praise Him over and over—ten times, a hundred times. *Praise You Jesus, praise You Christ.*

That's what will bring you joy because the Lord is joy personified.

If you are missing out on a blessed life, check to make sure it's not because you are still hooked into worldliness.

Money can't buy happiness and here we have the testimony of a former (wealthy) stockbroker, Albert Nastasi of

Pottsville, Pennsylvania, who, writing of that especially worldly occupation, said:

"The fast pace, high stress sales environment for retail stockbrokers is unimaginable. The rush of making easy money (often with just a phone call to a stranger) lured many unsuspecting young people looking for a high-paying career, and I was no different. I graduated in the top of my class with a degree in accounting, but was easily recruited by my friends to give up my accounting career to sell stocks and make big money.

"My first job as a stockbroker was in a small boiler room operation in New Jersey. When I first walked in, I saw about a hundred brokers all standing up, dialing the phones and speaking to strangers. We were taught to pretend we already spoke to the people we were calling. The story was that we left the potential investor with a stock pick six months prior; a winning recommendation that they could have bought and made tens of thousands of dollars on. We had no computers or research reports. We were only given phone numbers to dial, and we were usually told what to sell. In exchange we could make up to fifty percent commission on every dollar we brought in.

"Later that year, we moved our operation to Manhattan. The mystique of the city made us all feel like pros, even though nothing else had changed. Not too many of us realized what the potential consequences of our actions were. Sometimes the stocks went up a little and sometimes they went down; but we always made money.

"A few months after we moved into Manhattan, the Securities and Exchange Commission seized our records and shut us down (I later found out that the firm was a front for one of the New York crime families). Needless to say, I was devastated. I never realized this was possible. And because we were the only real market for the stocks we sold, almost every investor lost all of their money.

"In the years that followed, I worked for many different brokerage firms. Some of the firms were large world-renowned companies, and many were very small. However, no matter where I worked, the atmosphere and philosophy almost always remained the same. We opened accounts by selling stocks of very familiar large-cap companies, but once the account was opened, we often sold the highest commissioned stocks the firm had in inventory. Since 99 percent of sales were to people we never met, none of it seemed real; it never sank in; and I never thought of why I was able to make so much money.

"I remained a reckless stockbroker for seven years before I heard Our Lord's call to conversion.

"My conversion was very much a St. Paul conversion. I didn't believe in God or anything I could not see or feel. But in an instant, the Lord showed me there was much more. And in a couple of days, He showed me the depths of His love. My conversion took place on a cold night in February in a New York City after-hours club. I was dancing and interacting with some of the most unusual people I ever met. One couple even invited me to join them in a private room. The events that were going on in that room were very strange. Looking back now, I can only call it pure evil. In fact, I often wondered if some of the people may have been manifestations of evil: such as demons.

"As I was about to partake in the events of that room, I suddenly felt a force stopping me from moving forward. It was much like an invisible pair of hands keeping me out. Suddenly, I experienced what I can only now call an illumination of conscience. I was given to know all my sins and felt compelled to confess them right then and there. However, this force of grace stopped me. It was like my mouth was sewn shut. At the same time, I was also feeling a heightened sense of purity. The only thing my mind could equate this to was that I was to become a priest.

"I sat quietly and stunned for the rest of the night/morning. I watched what was happening around me with both great clarity and confusion. I was not used to this ultra sense of reality that included the grace to see beyond what was in front of me. It seemed I was living in a very vivid dream. I also felt sure that the world around me was about to end, and that I was going to somehow be left behind due to past pride and selfishness. The rest of that early Sunday morning, I experienced many humiliations with great peace and calm.

"After that evening, I slept for nearly two days. The following Wednesday morning, the first person I encountered had ashes on their forehead. *It was Ash Wednesday.* I instantly recognized that what was happening had to do with God. For some strange and special reason, God was calling me. It made me feel I was the only person in the world to Him, and that He loved me so much He was suspending time and all the natural laws to get my attention. I cried. Later that day, I rallied a dozen stockbrokers to go to Mass with me and get ashes. It was my first time back to Mass in over a decade. I even stayed around after Mass to make a confession, and I was in the confessional for more than a half an hour. When I read the Act of Contrition, I paused at the words, 'I will avoid whatever leads me to sin.' This struck me to the heart. In that moment, I knew I would never sell another stock again. In fact, I went back to my office, called my clients, and tendered my resignation.

"After my Confession, the priest told me about St. Faustina and the Divine Mercy devotion. He instructed me to buy St. Faustina's diary and see him again soon. While all this was going on, my father noticed the dramatic change in my life. He knew something happened to me, and as a loving father, he wanted to be by my side to see me through it. Even though he had been an agnostic most of his life, my father accompanied me to Palm Sunday Mass, and then to the Feast of Divine Mercy. We both made our Confession that day, but this time it was my father who took over a half an hour in the confessional. He had not been to Confession in many decades, and after his confession, he came out crying.

"Later that year, my father died of a sudden heart attack. There were no warning signs that he was sick. It was only for God to know, and apparently bringing my father back to the sacraments was all part of His plan. In fact, I believe my father was saved by God's awesome Mercy, and that he received this Mercy as a direct result of being so loving and merciful to his own son. My father took part in all of the Divine Mercy devotions that Sunday with me, and in Our Lord's own words, *'The soul that will go to Confession and receive Holy Communion shall obtain complete forgiveness of sins and punishment. On that day are opened all the Divine floodgates through which graces flow. Let no soul fear to draw near to Me, even though its sins be as scarlet.'*

"As an end note, my years of fast living led me into bankruptcy; and after quitting the stock market, I began a career as a Catholic high school math teacher. On this new path, the Lord allowed me to share his grace and touch many hearts with the story of His Mercy. I am now married to a devout Catholic woman, have two wonderful daughters, and I obtained my CPA. I still teach second-grade Catholic doctrine classes, which continually warms my heart; and my wife and I now attend daily Mass and are very active in spreading devotion to Our Lord's Divine Mercy and perpetual Adoration."

8

When We're Endlessly Blocked, it's Time to Cast Spirits Away in the Name of Jesus

We know when the Holy Spirit comes because we can feel peace and a *sense of well-being.*

"Oh Holy Spirit, come upon us. Come upon us with the richness of grace. Come upon us with healing. Come upon us to let us see with spiritual eyes. Come upon us in comfort and guidance.

"Oh come, Holy Spirit, and let us know how to tackle the issues in our lives."

If you are in any form of fear, cast it out. Get rid of it. That sounds easier said than done; sometimes it is. We're in a dark time. No one would deny it. But here's a simple but powerful truth: with sufficient prayer, all fear leaves.

When you're going into a situation that you fear or that may bring a fiery dart, say a prayer with faith and this will reduce the "zingers." You know how it is: every so often the devil sends you an antagonism. It can be in something someone does. It can be in what someone says. It can be in an e-mail. As soon as the sting comes, stop what you are doing and pray until the anger or fear or rejection in you passes. Step back from it. Get in the habit of this being your first reaction. Then you know you have the shield, and every time you do this, the shield will strengthen. It will become more effective. Soon, it will be impenetrable. The mistake we make is in reacting out of instinct, magnifying the darkness, and then ingesting negativity. If someone insults you or hurts you, say little about it. Talking often intensifies the sting. When we pray instead of dwelling on it, darkness leaves much sooner.

The same is true of fear. Fear is a great device of the devil, who likes to make himself look bigger than he really is. When you feel fear come, settle yourself into prayer and specifically command the *spirit of fear* away. "I command you, spirit of fear, by the power of God, in the Name of Jesus, to leave me and my surroundings and go to the foot of the cross to be disposed of according to the will of the Father. Never to return. Sealed against!" Try that next time fear comes. Try that next time a thought or news item or anything causes trepidation. Try it enough and the spirit of fear will become afraid of *you* and (if you pray enough) will never return. ("Sealed against!")

Are you blocked? Do you find yourself stymied despite prayer? Are you butting your head against a wall?

This especially happens when we seek to be healed. We just can't shake whatever it is that afflicts us. It doesn't seem to occur. Or, in our work, in our families, in our general lives, we seem predisposed to failure.

There is such a thing as redemptive suffering, but there are a lot of times that we block ourselves by believing our affliction is inevitable. In fact, there are many times— perhaps the majority of times—that it is *not* God's Will and instead comes from the enemy.

God is a healing God. He is the Lord of miracles. Much of our affliction comes from Satan. Time after time, Jesus cast demons out of those He intended to heal and this makes us know that many diseases as well as other problems are dealt with *once we realize that we are being blocked by a lack of faith, unconfessed sin, grudges we hold, and thus by the devil.* In speaking of healing, *James* 5:14 tells us to "confess your sins to one another and pray for one another, so that you will be healed." In *Psalms* (107:17) we are told, "Some were fools, suffering because of their sins and because of their evil." In *Jeremiah* 5:25 we hear that "your sins have kept these good things from you."

Sin blocks God's blessings!

Notes one Christian writer, Bill Banks: when we sin or lack love, when we harbor anger, "unforgiveness," or bitterness, when we have pride or an involvement in such things as pornography, materialism, and the occult, we expose ourselves to the agent of Satan, rather than to God, by such action.

We give the enemy a "legal right" to attack and gain a "stronghold" in our lives.

That can manifest physically.

As it says in *Ephesians* (4:26-27), "Be ye angry and sin not; let not the sun go down upon your wrath: *neither give place to the devil.*"

Through anger and pride we block God's blessings. In so doing we invite in the evil spirit, who, as Christ showed, is the destroyer: a murderer from the beginning, the spirit of affliction.

Name him. Cast him out by description. Throw the devil out in the Name of Jesus! Be sealed and healed.

If there is an intractable problem in your life, don't despair. Don't give up because prayers haven't "worked." You don't always have to be sick. It is not "inevitable." What you need to do is pray to the Holy Spirit to reveal what is blocking you and then cast that blockage out.

There are spirits of failure and spirits of distress and spirits of loneliness and phobias and spirits of just about anything negative. If you are in a snare and going around and around, if you are on a treadmill—if you can't break out of a negative cycle—*cast away the personal force* that may be blocking you. Do so during Mass. Do so while praying the Stations of the Cross. Do so while receiving the Precious Blood. (If it is a severe case, do so under the guidance of a priest.)

We all die, yes, but God wants you to have the *fullness of years* (however He designates that). He doesn't want you wasting away. When that happens, especially in youth, the focus must be on casting out the spirit of sickness. As Scripture indicates, such spirits can come through family lines, through our own darkness, and through the course of worldly interactions.

The prince of this world is Satan and Jesus came to defeat his works—among them infirmity. That's why we see in *Isaiah* 53: 4-5—in the prophecy of His Coming—that it says "through His stripes we are healed."

9

When Grace Arrives in an Instant: Telephoning God

Victory is encountered during prayer. It is encountered when we fast. It's encountered during the liturgy. Christ died for our sins and that implies He also died for our *infirmities*. He was and is the Great Healer. Notes *Matthew* 8:17, "He did this to make come true what the prophet Isaiah had said, 'He Himself took our sickness and carried away our diseases.'"

Clearly Christ came to heal; it is the devil who was "a murderer from the beginning." The Lord grants us life—and more abundantly (which has nothing to do with material wealth but everything to do with *well-being*).

That aspect is all but ignored in our times, when the secular has pervaded Christianity. Many Church leaders dismiss the gifts of deliverance and healing! Yet it is time to take Scripture seriously. "Bless the Lord, O my soul," says *Psalms* 103:2-3, "and forget not all his benefits: Who forgiveth all thine iniquities; Who healeth all thy diseases."

Michael Harold Brown

We have to believe even when the devil tries to steal away our faith. To get unblocked it is crucial to dispel fear and persist.

Fear often comes from the enemy; it leads to anti-blessings. "And we know that fear is not from the Lord. For God hath not given us the spirit of fear . . ." notes *2 Timothy* 1:7. "For the thing which I greatly feared is come upon me, and that which I was afraid of is come unto me," says *Job* 3:25.

When we get rid of fear—which may be the block—a whole new world opens before us (a world of brightness, a world of blessings, a world of wellness).

For some, purgatory is suffered here on earth. There are martyrs. Again, there is redemptive suffering. There was Job himself. Paul suffered a thorn in his side. Jesus demonstrated that there is suffering on this earth when He told us to carry our own crosses, daily. When He suffered, it was according to the Will (or "cup") of the Father.

But too often it's a simple block, not God's Will, that has caused us to be ill, and we need to get *un*blocked—believing in the power of God no matter what medical "experts" say.

If bad things keep happening, if there is block after block, if it is piling up, if there is one illness after another— if it all comes in the midst of other upheaval—it is probably the enemy at work and always remember your power in Christ to defeat him!

Cast out the spirit of this world *(I command all evil spirits away, in the Name of Jesus, I command all evil spirits away, I command all evil spirits away)*, persist with that, pray without ceasing, pray, pray, pray, fast—and watch how the Holy Spirit lifts blocks from you, including what is imprinted in your subconscious.

Want to feel a sudden infusion of grace? Want to surprise yourself with happiness? Dispel fear and stop complaining. You'll be astonished at how much closer God is when you're grateful than when you're in a state of dissatisfaction.

To complain means to grumble, to be annoyed, to express resentment. It's one thing to speak out when there are injustices or to report a serious situation. It's another to fear and complain.

When we complain—when we act like our lot in life is never good enough, when we are always declaring ourselves mistreated—we only give energy to whatever it is that is irritating us. Fear is faith in evil. Check this out: next time someone bothers or even insults you, suffer silence. Zip it. Don't mention it. Offer the silence up. Though it may cause a nettlesome aggravation for a short period of time, the "sting" will leave much sooner than if you complain about it!

Jesus never complained on the way to the Cross nor during the Crucifixion; His result Resurrection. So it is with us. The Lord told us to take up our crosses and often a cross is when something irritates us and we're tempted to voice anger.

While our psychologists tell us we need to "vent" negative emotions (and while there are times when we *do* need to express certain issues), for the most part "venting" makes an insult last that much longer.

Worst of all is when we complain about something we have prayed for. Think about this: We pray to get married and then complain about our husbands and wives! We pray for a job—and then, when we get it, we're full of complaints about it! We pray for kids—and then complain when we have to get up in the middle of the night!

This can be ingratitude, the opposite, of course, of thankfulness. It's a manifestation of pride. When we're resentful we believe we deserve better (indeed, that we deserve heaven on earth), and are indignant of anything less. That's pride and it's a good way of falling out of God's favor.

It never works. It compounds a bad situation. It's very counterproductive. Did Mary complain about how little she was given? Did Mary complain about the manger? Did she complain that she was having a Child in the most inconvenient of circumstances?

Instead of complaining we should be thanking God— and praising Him in all circumstances. Easier said than done? Yes. Much. We're all in this struggle called "life." It's one big test! There are constant aggravations. But when we pass the little quizzes along the way—when we make it over one of the countless obstacles, and when we offer up our silence—there is often an outpouring of grace. This is especially true when we are silent in the face of unfairness.

When we can do that—when we can dispel fear and shake off even something unfair—then grace is not only powerful and not only long-lasting but often arrives in an instant.

Now, join this with fasting.

Fasting is powerful because when we fast we are detaching ourselves from the world. This allows us to transcend the enemy.

We see that even Christ saw the need to fast before He set forth to conquer His foe. In detaching from the flesh, from the "kingdoms of the world," we rise above earthly spirits. This is why Scripture tells us there are certain spirits that are cast off only through prayer *and* fasting (*Matthew* 17:21).

There is tremendous power in fasting. There is spiritual protection. There is healing. There is discernment. We are less deceived when we fast; the spiritual landscape is clarified. It is also why the Virgin constantly urges fasting when she appears in apparition. For those who can, a great fast is bread and water, or perhaps just coffee or juice, for an entire twenty-four-hour day; for those who are infirm or elderly, a fast can be to forgo something we particularly like (a certain major food or something such as television, something significant).

We see in our time the many ways evil has cause sickness because it has not been challenged through fasting, which also purifies our bodies (and even causes our bodies to consume sickly cells). *"Renounce all passions and all inordinate desires,"* the Blessed Mother once said. *"Avoid television, particularly evil programs, excessive sports, the unreasonable enjoyment of food and drink, alcohol, tobacco."* With fasting, we find it easier to see the essential things of life, a famous priest once added. "In making us interiorly free, fasting makes it easier for us to move towards God," he said.

Many have fear because they are not fasting. Fasting removes fear. When we find ourselves in a difficult situation it is often because we have not fasted even though fasting is nearly as important as prayer. With fasting and faith anything and everything is possible (*Matthew* 17:20). Without it, fear can move in. *"The best fast is on bread and water,"* the Virgin said in one of her most remarkable messages. *"Through fasting and prayer one can stop wars, one can suspend the laws of nature."*

Suspend the laws of nature!

If you're afraid, fast and step up your prayer.

Pray from the heart. It's then that the Spirit comes. How can anything be scary when we have the Holy Spirit?

Don't get me wrong: tragedies must be mourned. The present hour is the most sobering since World War II and in my belief it's bound to get much more serious. Those who deny this—who don't think God chastises—must not believe in the Bible (see *Matthew* 24, or *Luke* 21; see the accounts of Noah and Jonah.)

But we *know* God is there, that after this life—no matter what might happen on earth—there is eternity.

Life never ends; the most horrible tragedy, the most spectacular death, is but a transition. And so merciful is God that we're told by those who have experienced clinical death that the Lord often takes a soul before the actual instant of impact. Death is often more frightening for those *watching* than those who are going through it. For them, there is no fear. There are deceased loved ones. There is the presence of saints. There are angels. It's when we're not spiritually prepared that we fear. And the best preparation is to grow in faith, love, and self-discipline (especially humility). Seek God. Forget worldliness. "If you are humble," said Mother Teresa, "nothing will touch you." If we are spiritually prepared, there is nothing to fear and there is the realization that some day in some way we all die and go on to a reality so exciting and vast it will take eternity to explore it!

"God has created us to love and to be loved, and this is the beginning of prayer—to know that He loves me, to know that I have been created for greater things," added Mother Teresa.

Those greater things are forever and they can not be terrorized or killed.

When we think of life in such terms it casts out fear and leads us to repentance. It's those short on faith who fall into a spiral of negative emotions. If you find yourself doing that, grab yourself by the bootstraps. Start anew. Don't obsess on your mistakes. It is the plea of faith that counts with God. We all know that. But do we remember it enough? Do we practice it sufficiently? When the going gets tough, the tough get praying. I speak here of *effective* prayer; prayer that works; prayer that leads to miracles.

There's the "telephone prayer." I used it recently while kayaking. Lost for several hours—with sunlight fading (and in a wildlife preserve rich with large alligators, water moccasins, and assorted other hazards)—I finally unleashed *a prayer from the heart* that was as simple as it was sincere.

Jesus, I trust in You. Mary, take over.

Area code. Telephone number.

That was repeated over and over and grew in power with each stroke of each paddle and suddenly we spotted a canal that materialized behind us and took us right to a bridge that led us to a boar-trapping camp where we not only got out of the swamp but found someone who against all odds got us and our kayak to our car (which was inside a wildlife management area that had closed for the day).

Any bookmaker would have bet we were going to be spending the night in that small boat, with no light, water, or cell phone.

God heard me. He hears all of us—and delights when we focus on prayer instead of panic (there was also a litany of saints).

That same week, at a local beach, a woman was swept out in a rip current and her boyfriend went out to try to save her. She couldn't swim. "The two then became separated and the man began to yell instructions to his 'frantic' girlfriend on how to get out of the rip current," reported the *St. Augustine Record*. "[A witness] said the woman told him she '*loudly prayed to God*' and was able to make it back to shore." Her friend, who could swim, did not make it back.

"Loudly" is from the heart, from the depth of being. Here you find God. It doesn't have to be an emergency. It simply has to be sincere.

Pray with your entire soul. Pray with your whole body.

It can be just a word or two. In fact, these are often the most effective. Remember His prayer from the Cross? *My God, My God . . .*

The area code is "Jesus I trust in You." Or just "Jesus, Jesus, Jesus."

Have you noticed how simple the requests were of those for whom Jesus worked healings?

God wants depth more than length. It's a matter of attitude. Look at a setback as a set up (for a comeback). Instill yourself with *holy determination*. Pray as if you *are* desperate—but full of faith.

Don't complain.

Aim for what you need.

Holy determination knows no discouragement. It replaces anxiety with a novena.

Crises are bumps in the road (maybe speed bumps; maybe you need to slow down!) but winter always turns to spring. "This too shall pass" is crucial to dealing with our journeys on earth.

There are seasons of trial. There are seasons of favor. An unanswered prayer is a prayer that is not yet in season.

Eyes of faith see that.

They also see the new season.

Believe that.

Desire nothing (selfish); you will possess everything.

"Mary take over. Jesus. Jesus."

Those are some hints through the ages.

10

Chasing Away the Devil

Here is another hint: laughter chases the devil away. He hates when we laugh because when we laugh we have joy. The devil is the antithesis of that.

"Laugh and grow strong," said St. Ignatius Loyola.

One night I heard a preacher talk about how the devil tries to emotionally block us up like throwing stones in a well. He does this our entire lives. Laughter is like a geyser that tosses the boulders aside. It lets loose healing. It releases hormones called endorphins (which cause us to relax).

True, there's nowhere in Scripture where Christ told a joke. And, true, earth is serious business. I'd never deny that! I'm cognizant of the dangers and difficulties on earth. No one could accuse me of taking such things lightly.

But we need to have joy. We need to have balance. No matter the difficulty, the bottom line is that we live forever—eternity is a fact—and knowing this should expel all gloominess.

Want to say an effective prayer? Pray for a better sense of humor. Pray for a smile. Pray to make others laugh. You'll be amazed at how quickly the Holy Spirit will move in this direction, for God has a very cheerful side. His deepest essence is joy. Pray to lift your spirits. Pray to lift the spirits of *others*.

When we do, the devil flees because with good humor comes the light of Heaven.

If we are humble and have faith there is no room for fear.

Love casts out fear and leads us to humbleness which drives the enemy away.

As St. Thérèse of Lisieux said, "The nature of love is to humble oneself."

It is when we have pride that we fear. It's when we don't pray. It's when we bear jealousy or animosity or hatred. With prayer there is nothing to fear because with prayer we can prevent war; like I said, we can suspend natural laws!

And if our souls are pure, what, in the grand scheme of eternity, can harm us?

With purity, no event on earth, no assault, can prevent us from reaching heaven.

This is not to deny the presence of demons. We have never seen more evil. This is the full-fledged assault that we have been expecting. Satan is becoming very aggressive. He knows he must move fast. His power will soon diminish.

But we don't fear him because fear is faith in the devil and can unleash his power.

Instead, we fear only God and have faith that He will protect us.

It really is a remarkable time—daunting, perhaps, and sad, but exciting at a spiritual level. We were all set on this earth at this moment to battle for God. That's exciting. "Just as the sun shines simultaneously on the tall cedars and on each little flower as though it were alone on the earth, so

Our Lord is occupied particularly with each soul as though there were no others like it," St. Thérèse assured us.

You are protected. God knows everything you need. He is watching over you and your loved ones—He is watching over our nation, which He wants (in His mercy) to purify. As Thérèse wrote: for His most intimate friends, God works no miracles before testing their faith. At Cana Christ said His hour had not yet come when first they wanted wine, but after that initial test, the water was changed into wine (just as the Virgin, who we should all implore, had requested).

"I love You and I give myself to You forever!" Thérèse shouted to Christ—Who in His time answers all prayers.

"O Jesus, my Beloved, Who could express the tenderness and sweetness with which You are guiding my soul!" said Thérèse. "It pleases You to cause the rays of Your grace to shine through even in the midst of the darkest storm!"

Remember that if God was the Empire State Building, the devil, in comparison, would be smaller than a grain of sand.

Yet, when we have pride or any darkness we grant him a "legal" right to a certain part of our terrain.

When we're tempted to sin, it often comes in the way of a thought from him. He's trying to get that foothold. It isn't just our flesh. There are real entities that send us unholy thoughts (while on the other shoulder, angels send good ones). The bad thoughts are called "temptations," and it's not just *having* the thought that gets us into trouble. It's not the first one. It's willingly having such a thought, or hanging onto one. God may excuse the first tempting thought; we're held accountable when we don't dispel them.

We can look to an old Cherokee who was teaching his grandson about life. "A fight is going on inside me," he said to the boy. "It is a terrible fight and it is between two wolves. One is evil—he is anger, envy, sorrow, regret, greed, arrogance, self-pity, guilt, resentment, inferiority, lies, false pride, superiority, and ego." He continued, "The other is good—he is joy, peace, love, hope, serenity, humility, kindness, benevolence, empathy, generosity, truth, compassion, and faith. The same fight is going on inside you—and inside every other person, too." The grandson thought about it for a minute and then asked his grandfather, "Which wolf will win?" The old Cherokee simply replied, "The one you feed."

Anger. Lust. Jealousy. When we make such a choice—when we allow a sinful idea to repeat in our minds—it becomes entrenched. A brief thought of aggravation may develop into anger which develops into a tirade! Or, a quick thought of envy may turn into full-blown jealousy (and if we keep dwelling on it: hatred). A lustful thought becomes a fantasy that tempts us to pornography, fornication, and even adultery.

When we go yet further and verbalize such thoughts—discuss them aloud—they are enhanced geometrically.

And pretty soon, eradicating the thought seems next to impossible. They're like what they call "sand-diggers"—little crabs that scurry into the sand along the ocean. Wrong thoughts scurry quickly into the sands of the psyche and pretty soon we can't get them out.

Sin likes darkness because it is in the dark that it multiplies.

Thus, one key to holiness and blessings is to watch every single thought. If bad ones keep repeating, head for the sacraments. Go to Confession. That sacrament has a wondrous effect on freeing us from harmful patterns of thought, for when we confess, we shed light into the darkness and feel an actual release from thoughts that have haunted us.

We start with a clean slate.

And it becomes easier to resist the next temptation.

This is all crucial because when we die we'll be held accountable not only for everything we have done or everything we have said, but for everything we have *thought* (or at least each bad thought that we have clung to).

So stop every little fiery dart and halt temptation at its first hint. Don't let the sand-digger dig. If there's a thought of lust, quench it with one of holiness, and if there's a thought of anger, quench it with love.

This is what the Bible calls resisting the devil—and like the Good Book says, when we resist him long enough, he finally gives up.

11

Invoke the Holy Spirit and Take Time to be Personal

Resisting the devil means invoking the Holy Spirit. He has domain over all! Among the countless lessons of John Paul II was the ease with which the Holy Spirit operates when we have a personal touch and when what we're doing is in God's Plan.

Let's take a quick look at John Paul (the Great):

He was not a man who aspired to the papacy; in fact, there are those who believe he was tempted to turn it down in favor of a monastic life. He wasn't obsessed with "success"; he certainly was not competitive. The papacy was something for which he neither strained nor politicked.

Diligent, yes: to the maximum. But not obsessed with his own success.

Karol Wojtyla performed his duties with maximum obedience and left the rest to God.

The same with Pope Benedict XVI. He said he even prayed *not* to be made Pope. The papacy followed him because it was in God's Plan.

It's funny in our own lives how good things follow us— almost pursue us—when we don't lust after them.

If we're yearning for something or straining too hard toward a goal, it's usually something we want and not something that God has in mind for us. It's time for all of us to realize this and tune in more carefully to what the Lord has designed as our true stations in life. Otherwise, we throw our personal lives into turmoil.

These are important words: "true station" in life. We live at a time when everyone wants to be a "big shot." But true contentment comes only when we seek the big in the small and fit into the role that God has designed for us.

Work hard, yes, but don't get obsessed or hyper; don't force things; and don't neglect the truly important things like friends and family. If there is frenzy in your life, halt what you're doing and ask God to tell you if your wants—your plans (as opposed to His)—are causing the tension.

These days we're experts at causing tension and letting life go by without appreciating what is precious. Don't we all make mountains out of mole hills? Don't we all fall into the temptation of overly complicating things?

No matter what you do in life, if you want to, you can make it tense.

Think about it a moment:

In what ways do you create your own tension? What do you demand of yourself each morning? Are you overly rigid? Do you set forth a schedule that has no time for other people, for the truly important things in life—no flexibility—and then panic when events punch holes in that plan?

If so, it's because you want to be in control instead of letting God control the events in your life; you are reaching beyond your true zone of comfort.

When we're tense, something is off center. To find out what it is, we have to seek the Holy Spirit. He will reveal what we're doing (or not doing) that is leading to the feeling of being on edge.

It could be jealousy. It could be a sense of competition. It almost always goes back to pride. If you dig to the root of many tensions, it comes from comparing yourself to others.

That creates stress because competition, which is based on pride, is not in God's Plan. It alienates us from others when what we're supposed to be doing is nurturing relationships. Note that Christ did not line up His disciples and set them off to the races. He placed them together, not against each other.

When you are as concerned about others as yourself and take time to be a *person* (not a "success machine"), this alone will diminish your stress.

Christ is the Prince of Peace and does not want you on the edge about anything. He wants you securely in His arms. But we have to seek His arms, and we have to approach life the way He did. That means handing the "cup" over to God, and—like John Paul II—letting Him set the schedule.

When things in your life seem almost too much to handle, when twenty-four hours in a day are not sufficient, remember the mayonnaise jar and the two cups of coffee:

As the story goes, a professor stood before his philosophy class and had some items in front of him. When the class began, he silently picked up a very large empty mayonnaise jar and proceeded to fill it with golf balls. He then asked the students if the jar was full.

They all agreed that it was.

The professor then picked up a box of pebbles and poured them into the jar, shaking it lightly.

The pebbles rolled into the open areas between the golf balls.

He then asked the students again if the jar was full. They agreed it was.

Next the professor picked up a box of sand and poured that into the jar. Of course, the sand filled up the remaining space. He asked once more if the jar was full. The students responded with a unanimous "yes."

He then produced two cups of coffee from under the table and poured the entire contents into the jar, effectively filling the empty space between the sand. The students laughed.

"Now," said the professor, as the laughter subsided, "I want you to recognize that this jar represents your life.

"The golf balls are the important things—God, family, your children, your health, your friends, and your favorite passions—things that if everything else was lost and only they remained, your life would still be full.

"The pebbles are the other things that matter like your job, your house, and your car.

"The sand is everything else—the small stuff.

"If you put the sand into the jar first," he continued, "there is no room for the pebbles or the golf balls. The same goes for life. If you spend all your time and energy on the small stuff, you will never have room for the things that are important to you.

"Pay attention to the things that are critical to your happiness.

"Play with your children.

"Take your partner out to dinner.

"Play another 18.

"There will always be time to clean the house and fix the disposal.

"Take care of the golf balls first, the things that really matter. Set your priorities.

"The rest is just sand."

One of the students raised her hand and inquired about what the coffee represented.

The professor smiled. "I'm glad you asked. It just goes to show you that no matter how full your life may seem, there's always room for a couple of cups of coffee with a friend."

12

Detach From the World and It Will Quench 'Fire'

Detach from what is unimportant. Purify. Seek to cleanse through the immaculate help of Mary.

That Our Blessed Mother was immaculate—that she was born without the taint of original sin—was confirmed during apparitions at the southern end of France in the range of mountains known as the Pyrenees. We can't be sure we know all the details, for the seer, Saint Bernadette Soubirous, was a very private person. We do know that the main part of her experience occurred between February and July of 1858 when Mary appeared eighteen times to her.

This was in a small cave or grotto along the River Gave at the city of Lourdes. Bernadette was out looking for firewood with her sister and a friend when the visitations occurred. She was a humble girl hailing from a destitute family that was so poor it could not even afford a house; they found quarters in a donated hovel that once had been the local *cachot* (or jail).

So cramped were the quarters in which Bernadette lived that for a time she was sent to live with a family that employed her as a shepherdess.

Most of you know the story. It was there that she called herself the "Immaculate Conception," confirming a new Church dogma.

"Pray for sinners," the Virgin said to Bernadette, underlining the serious nature of life and how we must always watch over our own conduct, as well as help other people by praying for their conversion.

We are people of God, and when one sinner—just a single sinner—is brought back to the fold, the entire universe is positively affected.

"Penitence," Mary had also said at Lourdes—indicating how important it is for all of us to meditate on our faults and atone for them while we're still on earth.

"Penitence, penitence."

This is so important you will hear me repeat it.

The more we purify ourselves during life—the more we pray and sacrifice—the less time we will have to spend in Purgatory.

Above all, strive to have Jesus in your heart.

He is the essence of purity. He is the Light.

During another Church-approved apparition, at Kibeho, in Rwanda, the dear Blessed Mother said, "All of you who are sick with incurable sicknesses, a good heart surpasses all; there are no riches that are beyond a clean heart.

"All of you who have had difficulties of all kinds; there are difficulties everywhere, in all walks of life. When they don't go away, offer them to God.

"Every good Christian is requested to offer a sacrifice. All of you who have problems in your families; think of the Holy Family, who [like Bernadette] lived in such poverty, and who lived among those who didn't like them nor understand them, and with the problems you have, come close to [the Holy Family]. All of you who have dedicated your lives to God, a life like that is not easy: the most important thing is to be faithful to your promises."

It is in praying the Rosary of the Seven Sorrows of the Virgin Mary (it was said at Kibeho) that we maintain joy— and can achieve *self-illumination*.

"During her visitations to Kibeho, the Holy Virgin revealed that this Rosary possesses immense spiritual power for those who say it sincerely," wrote a Rwandan woman whose mission it is to promote Kibeho and the Rosary. "She promised that when prayed with an open and repentant heart, the Rosary would win us the Lord's forgiveness for our sins and free our souls from guilt and remorse.

"She also promised that over time, the Rosary would develop within us a deep understanding of why we sin, and that this knowledge would give us the wisdom and strength to change or remove any internal flaws, weaknesses of character, or personality faults causing unhappiness and keeping us from the joyous life God intended for us to live."

When one is pure, the devil has no claim to your territory.

At Lourdes, Mary showed herself as immaculate, and those who follow her are shielded from temptation; we are cleansed. It's no idle fact that during the apparitions Bernadette was transformed into radiant beauty; purity beautifies. To enjoy such "illumination" (visible blessing), we must do our part in detaching from the things of this world. Mary told Bernadette she could not promise happiness in this world, only in the next. Mary wants us to divorce ourselves from materialism.

Thus we contemplate the importance of always remembering that earth is a temporary place and we are in exile. *"Detach, detach, detach"* was as much the message from Lourdes as *"penitence, penitence, penitence."*

The less worldly you are, the less prone to the darts of the enemy.

That's because when you rise above worldliness—its judgments, its competitions, its standards—you perceive differently. You're less "bugged" by things that would have riled you otherwise.

You know what I mean. You have gone through it. Odds are, you are still going through it: someone somewhere in your life—a relative, a neighbor, a co-worker, perhaps a fellow worshipper—is the source of constant aggravation.

Call them "fiery arrows": There is just something so galling about it! All of us have people who have attacked us unfairly and sometimes viciously out of their own misconceptions (or demons).

It makes us angry! Yet, here is a lesson: See it from a distance. All it takes to overcome anger is to step back and rise above it—watching the scenes that anger as if you are at a theater watching a play on a stage.

When we react in the wrong way to an insult, when we "counter-punch," when we retaliate (through anger), the hissing serpent has his way. Scripture tells us this when it says, "Be ye angry and sin not; let not the sun go down on your wrath; neither give place to the devil" (in *Ephesians* 4:26-27).

To *feel* anger is not a sin; what is a sin is to handle it in the wrong manner.

It's natural to get angry when evil is done! But when we react wrongfully, when we don't detach, as I mentioned earlier, we empower the venom.

If you see something wrong, step back, disengage your emotions, pray about how to approach it, and then seek with love (sometimes tough love) to correct it.

That removes the sting. Is it difficult? Sometimes it seems impossible! But we are called to do it and we are called to do it at times when we least want to—which, if and when we pass the test, increases the blessings.

Christians have a duty to "oppose evil with good, lies with the truth, and hatred with love," Pope Benedict XVI said in an Ash Wednesday homily.

But it is in the way we do it—and we react in the wrong way when we let pride speak for us.

Negativity drains energy while the power of love (and humility) sends correction.

How powerful that is!

Correction is seeking to make something good; it is responding to anger in the correct way; it's using love to buffer oneself from a negative situation.

The key is love, which is a shield against evil and allows us to say something without offending. If we love, we correct. If we love, we detach from emotions that interfere with that love. It's hard to love both the world and God at the same time. We can't serve two masters.

Said with charity, our voices can affect the world. And our love can keep the snakes away (see Saint Patrick). When we do not shine light, there is dark.

13

The Force of Forgiveness

Now let's take this a step further—to forgiveness. Few things are more important in "detaching"! You don't want to be bound to a person of this earth and their negativity. When you carry a grudge, that's what occurs.

Forgive, forgive, forgive, forgive.

When asked how often we should forgive someone, Jesus said not seven times, but *seventy times seven*. We don't often think of how important forgiveness is, but it's crucial in setting ourselves emotionally free.

Those who have glimpsed eternity say total forgiveness is required before we are pure enough to don the white robes of Heaven. During a vision of Heaven Teresa of Avila said, "I saw myself being clothed in a garment of great whiteness and brightness. At first I could not see who was clothing me, but later I saw Our Lady on my right hand and my father St. Joseph on my left, and it was they who were putting the garment on me." She described the brightness as "a radiance which dazzles, but a soft whiteness and an infused radiance which, without wearying the eyes, cause them the greatest delight. So *different from any earthly light* is the brightness and light now revealed to the eyes that, by comparison with it, the brightness of our sun seems quite dim." This is the brightness to which we must aspire.

From it come blessings.

"When a person is unforgiving," writes charismatic priest Father Robert DeGrandis, "there are spiritual chains around him, and they are also around the person who is not forgiven. Both people involved are in bondage." There is also darkness.

Think about that: when we hold on to unforgiveness— when we maintain a grudge—we're in an unhealthy *bond* with the person who has hurt us. We're actually tied to her or him. "You must forgive, otherwise your heavenly Father cannot forgive you because you are holding back the Spirit," said Father DeGrandis. "You are blocking the flow of the Spirit, closing the door. You are willingly staying in the dark and not entering into the Light."

That blocks healing, says Father Degrandis. He suggested that we all should go deeply into prayer and ask the Holy Spirit to reveal all the people we need to forgive. One good way of doing this is through what Father DeGrandis calls "The Forgiveness Prayer" [*see appendix*]. It is based on a simple precept: Through life, we gather a long list of friends, relatives, and acquaintances we need to forgive. In prayer, we will know how to do this. When you pray, you'll be amazed how many things will come to mind. Start with your earliest memories and take a prayerful walk through your life. As soon as a person you need to forgive pops into your consciousness, forgive that person; resolve not to think again of the offense; *pray* for him. This is what Jesus did right from the Cross—and there is nothing that sets us free quicker.

There's the need to forgive friends. There is the need to forgive enemies. There is the need to forgive our closest relatives. A friend once related how a Viet Nam veteran who had been an army sniper was suffering horrible night terrors that eased only when he began to forgive all involved in Viet Nam—including the Viet Cong who had once put quite a scare into him. This loosed blessings in the way of sudden demonstrations of appreciation from various folks for his service (he had felt much neglected). "When we harbor bitterness, resentment, and unforgiveness, we are in effect inviting the devil to become involved in our lives," noted Father DeGrandis (a world-traveling evangelist). "Families and countries have been split apart by unforgiveness, bitterness, resentment, and hatred. I firmly believe this can open people up to demonic activity. If we have been wounded and will not forgive, we deepen our wounds. When we forgive another we who have been wounded become the channel for healing."

That's because resentment and unforgiveness are scar tissue that blocks the flow of the Lord's love into our lives. When we forgive, which is to love (often through detachment from the negative), we see remarkable changes in our lives—sometimes gradually, sometimes in a way that's miraculous. Father DeGrandis cited the case of a woman who prayed the "forgiveness prayer" for seven days and saw a lump in her neck disappear.

Another recovered from facial paralysis.

"Following the guidance that the Lord had revealed to us, we began to enter into a prayer for forgiveness at the beginning of each healing session, and we saw tremendous breakthroughs," said the priest. "During these sessions we have seen cases where, although the pain did not leave when the person was prayed for, it disappeared completely when the 'prayer for forgiveness' was said."

Is there a problem in your life that won't go away? Is there blockage? Is there something emotionally troubling you—even a serious physical ailment?

14

The Real You

You are not blessed to fulfill the mission God has given you unless you seek purity along the way and are *yourself*, the way He intended you to be.

God intends some of us to be mailmen and some congressmen and some housewives and in the end He judges on how well we did what He set for us to do, how we handled our missions. Too often, we orient everything to what others will think when we shouldn't care about that. We should care about what heaven thinks. And that judgment is different than the way things are viewed from here (where physical allurements confuse those who seek to materialism).

When we are ourselves, we are closest to God because God made us and when we allow Him to orient us, when we allow Him to materialize our plans—when we *let go*—we have His happiness. What joy to simply walk the path that He set! What a joy to ignore the competition of a world that is blinded by the flesh! What a joy to rise above the judgments of those obsessed with attaining things that in the end they can't keep.

When we die, God will judge in great part on how close we ended our lives to what He intended as well as how much we loved. Were we terrific, spiritual housewives, great fathers, spiritual mailmen who spread His example, who worked in the places He had positioned us—or did we try to attain things because we aimed for societal stature? Were we good at housework, plumbing, rearing children—or did we force ourselves into "prestigious" occupations that were never designated for us? Did we preach His word or were we afraid of what others might think?

One of the wisest things we can realize is that whatever role God assigned us is as important as any other in the scheme of eternity. We're all equal. And we have to put God's desires above all others. This is crucial: not caring how we are viewed by others and instead seeking the happiness that God grants those who carry forth the mission He has designated.

Doing that means looking in the mirror and not worrying about how others view us but asking *Him* what we should be.

Tie that with discipline.

"Discipline is the key to happiness" is an old adage and while there are other things as important, we can see the truth: when we have discipline we have joy because discipline leads to many blessings.

Meditate on the life of Jesus. He was the personification of discipline. He had the discipline to fast for forty days. He had the wherewithal to bear others. He had the discipline to avoid sin. It was discipline that prepared Him for that flurry of miracles and allowed Him to defeat evil; it was discipline that propelled His *disciples*.

That's because discipline leads to self-control and faith and when we have that we improve spiritually, emotionally, and even *physically*. We gain respect. We gain in love. Discipline conquers all because it is ready for anything.

Does not discipline determine what we eat? Does it not determine how we react to others? Does it not determine how much time we set aside for meditation and love and prayer (as opposed to how much time we set aside for watching TV)?

Discipline means setting aside the time to pray.

It means watching over one's interior life.

It means contemplation.

How do we start?

By developing a "do-it-now" attitude: When something needs to be done, we should do it right away. The enemy of discipline is procrastination. Make it a mantra: do it now, do it now, do it now.

Instead of letting things build up (and haunt you), start this moment with an attitude of picking up something that needs to be picked up as soon as you approach it—not after you've passed it a dozen times. Develop the habit of praying right away (and first thing in the morning). Develop the habit of tackling hard tasks right away.

It also means *organization*. Making a list of things we have to do organizes our minds and takes away the burden of having to remember everything, which also diminishes our anxiety. It's astonishing how peaceful our lives can become and how much we accomplish when we're organized. An organized mind operates in a maximum way, and that's something we all need to work on. Discipline maximizes spiritual gifts.

When we don't discipline ourselves, God does it for us (in ways we don't always like).

So make a list. Tackle what you least like first. Get the basic work done—and watch your ease develop. Watch your happiness grow. Watch how you begin to enjoy much more in life—*even the process* of discipline!

15

Joy Comes Even From Sadness, if We Persevere

Apply discipline to perseverance.

Another lesson of Mary—as Our Lady of Sorrows—is that from disaster can come happiness and joy from grief. It's up to you. It's a matter of persevering.

Mary didn't run away from the Cross. She did not avoid the greatest personal calamity anyone could endure. She didn't choose to shield her eyes as her Son was crucified.

The Blessed Virgin Mary persevered to the end and in short order was witness to the greatest event in history.

As a result, all generations will call her "blessed" and so too are we blessed when we persevere. If we detach ourselves from negative emotions there is always glory after sadness. It's up to us to make the cycle of gloom a short one!

For such are the trials of life that we have good times and bad times, excellent days and ones that are awful. Yet equally true is the rule that *from disaster is always the potential for something good.*

Such is true whether in huge calamities like Hurricane Katrina or issues in our personal lives: When God allows disaster, He is clearing brush, hauling away the rubble, and offering us space for restructuring.

Sorrow, yes; we experience that; the Blessed Mother did. But her sorrow was never morbid (or obsessive). It was not morbid (as we see too often at funeral homes). It was not a depression that lingered. It did not equal despair.

A bad fruit this is, despair.

For we despair only when we lose sight of Heaven—and *Mary never lost sight of the supernatural.*

That only happens when—once more—we overly focus on things of this world. We despair when we listen too much to what the world has to say. It is the world that sees only the physical. It is the world that tells us to lament. It is the world that loses sight of Heaven. It is the world that tries to make one person more important than the next (causing despair this way also).

To detach from that is to transcend it—*and to transcend sorrow along with it!*

Do you care what kind of car a neighbor drives? Do you care what society thinks of you? Do you follow the secular news as the definition of reality?

Do you still read more secular than spiritual material (more in the way of newspapers than in the way of Holy Scripture)?

It is the judgment of the material, human-centered, egoistic world that causes spiritual vacancy (and vagrancy). It is also the judgment of the world that leads us to jealousy. It is the judgment of the world that brings over-sadness.

When we're suffering those things, it's frequently because we still have not shaken the attitude of the world—which wants us to put man in the place of God and live as if earth is the final destination.

Sadness lingers only when we hold too desperately onto something and view it with worldly eyes instead of lifting them to Heaven.

Ask the Blessed Mother!

After the Sorrowful Mysteries come the Glorious ones.

That's her Rosary, and with it sadness vanishes.

To persevere is to have faith. Faith builds upon faith. That is, for faith to grow, it must be exercised, and we have to be faithful first in small things. We need positive internal dialogue (or "self-talk"). We have to think the best, as did Mary.

And we need to pray with *specificity*. Envision the end result and pray for all aspects and details of what you seek. Don't just throw off prayers. Don't just glance over matters. Pray from the heart for every detail until you have tranquility. The more you pray, the more God answers, and the more He answers what seem like those little prayers—those prayers about small matters in life, those requests for everyday assistance, those constant supplications about our jobs and children and even a traffic light—the more your faith increases.

This is how faith works and builds and how miracles begin.

We roll a little ball down a mountain and it grows into a bigger ball—until we can move the mountain itself.

If we build up faith like we build up our muscles we'll get to the point of astonishing strength. Didn't Christ say that? It wasn't hyperbole. In Florida, prayer groups have prayed away storms and hermits in Nebraska prayed away a tornado that suddenly lifted from its direct path toward them and in California the Big One has not yet come in part due (I am convinced) to those who have unfailingly prayed over that fault known as the San Andreas (of course, some day it may let go). Want a mountain? Monsignor Salvatore

Gristina, an archbishop in Italy, once went up Mount Etna, Europe's highest volcano, when its eruption jeopardized neighboring buildings. For weeks the lava had been posing a dire threat, but only five hours after his benediction the flow suddenly veered off course.

"'Divine intervention' diverts Etna lava," said a headline in England's *Daily Telegraph*,

Fantasy?

Faith can do *anything*.

How do we start?

As with every other attribute, the way to increase faith is to constantly practice. When we use what we have and *all* of what we have, faith grows; we receive more; it is a tightened, larger "blessing" muscle. To use another metaphor, developing faith is like planting seeds. Mustard seeds. Those are among the tiniest seeds, but when nurtured they grow into an awesome tree, the roots of which can split rocks beneath it, the bark of which is impenetrable, and the branches of which reach heavenward. If you want to crack open a mountain, plant mustard seeds on top of it!

Any time we have faith, we are *blessed*. If we plant enough seeds, there will be a "harvest." And the better we become at it, the larger our harvest will become. Even if some of the things in which we have faith don't pan out—even if certain prayers aren't "answered"—we'll still receive benefits. It may have seemed like an unanswered prayer—like we wasted faith—but that's never true. God knows when we have done something in faithfulness. *He* knows when we have held hope despite all the odds. He may not answer in the way we want, but if so, it's because it is not the time; it is not in His plan for us; it's not what is *best* for us.

But it still goes into what can be likened to a spiritual bank account.

God keeps track of our faithfulness and adds "interest" each time we exercise it.

Once we identify a problem in our lives, we should verbalize its remedy. We do this in prayer—removing thoughts of illness and failure. If it is right for us that the prayer be answered, then God will work the miracle. It is not to deny the presence of a problem; we don't hide our heads in the sand. And we certainly don't lie to ourselves. But we *do* deny the power of a problem over our divine right to remove it.

We have the right.

That's how good God is.

When we practice faith in both small and large things, when we are constant, and when we never allow discouragement, we can expect a large blessing. Sometimes, it takes a while; sometimes, it comes in a gradual fashion. But it comes. It is *inevitable*. No exercise of faith is ever wasted. If we maintain faith in all things—if we keep exercising it, tossing those seeds, it's only a matter of time before a big prayer is answered.

At other times, God simply shines down upon us—in His Mercy.

I heard from a woman named Stacie in Florida, who was both a local businesswoman and drug abuser when she lost her timepiece—a $2,000 Tag Heuer designer watch—on a beach just off the coast in the gorgeous Gulf of Mexico across from Sanibel Island. Let's take a look at this "coincidence."

"Drug abuser" meant "crystal meth," or what is known in common parlance as "ice": a stimulant that grants a false sense of euphoria but leads to insomnia and paranoia and—as Stacie will attest—lifelessness.

Her world had been falling apart. She and her husband were doing well financially—she had all kinds of clothes, all the accoutrements, all the "toys"—but she had been a drug user since the ninth grade and still had not kicked it—could not kick it. "I was a drug fiend my whole life," she says. "I tried every drug. I would do drugs for six months, then go into rehab. I rehabbed six times."

Then came the "event."

It was the summer of 2003 when the watch went missing. "That day we were out on our jet skiis and I got stuck in the mud," says Stacie. "When I got back, I realized that I had lost my watch."

The narcotics went on. The fast lane continued. She was going through a drug "hell." Nine months into a stupor, the following January, she and her husband were staying at a bed-and-breakfast that they later bought and she was feeling a peculiar presence around her; she wasn't sure what it was. It started to make her paranoid. She felt something and stopped doing the drug (wondering if it was responsible for the feeling) and yet it wouldn't go away.

"We had gotten a brand new boat, put it in water, and headed out to this island, but the presence never left me," said Stacie, freely offering her incredible testimony.

"Suddenly I turned right with the boat. I didn't know why. I had been beelining for the island and suddenly took a right and I thought, 'Why am I doing this? What is going on? What: does God want me here?' I was zig-zagging in and out of mangroves and I hit this sand bar. I came to a spot where there was a sandbar and my boat stopped. And I saw a reflection, like a jewel."

There on the exposed sand was her Tag Heuer designer watch—four miles from where she had lost it nine months earlier!

The tide had taken it out. God had done the rest.

"There was my watch sitting on the sandbar!" recalled Stacie, who is now a devout Catholic. "The thought then came to me, like a message, All in good time. If you take an 'o' out of 'good' you've got 'God.'"

A lesson there. Several lessons! It was like a bolt of lightning. It was Stacie's "road-to-Damascus" experience.

Moreover, the watch was still ticking. "It still worked," says Stacie, "and the date was correct."

"From that day forward, I threw away everything that attached me to the old Stacie," she says. "We renewed our wedding vows. I started to go to daily Mass. The Holy Spirit—I could feel Him in me. I became a Holy Spirit robot. I stopped cursing. It was a miracle. I never did drugs again after that."

Raised Catholic, and educated in Catholic schools—one of nine children—she had come back, blessed, from the land of the dead.

16

Back From the Land of the Dead (and Dark)

As the saying goes, the darkest moment is often just before dawn (unless we hold onto the darkness). Anxiety solves nothing and spoils everything. Tribulation should lead to new ways of viewing life, which leads to joy, the emotion of miracles, along with love (which *causes* joy).

God is love. God is joy. There you have a key to life. Difficulty opens us to love.

And handled well, suffering leads to resurrection.

When we let Him, God comes to our rescue, whatever our stations in life, whatever our circumstances, and whatever the hour. All of us have dark moments whether in relationships, finances, or health. When we learn to have faith in the midst of it and correct imperfection, God swoops in and lifts the oppression.

He is always there!

When we *don't* recognize our faults—when we don't get down on our knees, and stay there, repenting, looking to the Sacred Heart (during a disturbance in life)—problems grow more severe.

Those who get legalistic lack miracles because they are so immersed in the minutiae of religion that the soil they till becomes hardened clay.

We have to *ardently*, directly, seek God; the more direct we are with Him, the quicker He responds.

Think of times when you have been in crisis. How did you pray then? If your requests poured from your being, if you prayed from the bottom of your soul, and if you felt a surrender, then you prayed with your heart.

This is crucial.

If you could pray that way every time, you'd be loaded with blessings.

Prayer from the heart is openness to God and even the environment responds around us (as in, "green thumb"). *Any miracle is possible.*

In conformance with Christ, we prosper. He can make something from nothing.

I don't think there's a better example than the poor people of Juarez, Mexico.

Many of them are what they call "trash grubbers." Surviving on what they find at a local dump, they live in vast barrios with no electricity, sanitation, or running water. There is no such thing as welfare. They don't need it. They are recipients of miracles right out of the Bible. It started back in Christmas of 1972 when a charismatic prayer group led by Father Richard Thomas decided to prepare dinner for the indigents. From eleven a.m. until late afternoon, they did just that, organizing a charitable meal. Everyone received a generous share. In fact, there was food left over.

What was unusual is that Father Thomas's group had prepared for only one hundred and fifty people—*not the three hundred* who came and *even had seconds.*

Those cutting the meat felt as if it was maintaining the same size even as they sliced off portions.

With God, anything is possible.

Time and again, this would happen when Father Thomas and his group were ministering to the poor. There was the miracle of multiplication.

These people were in their darkest moment—at least as the world measures it. They had no one to feed them. They were at the end of the rope. They literally dug for meals—even on Christmas. And now God was sending them *manna*. Bible miracles are true and occur in our present day when we look for them.

God multiplies in all our lives but does so in ways that seem so natural we take it for just that.

Almost everyone has known times when the right amount of money came at just the right time.

When God is close, there is all we need. This also occurred to Bob Rice, the former truck driver who reported healings. Serving as a Eucharistic minister during a visit to a church in Damascus, Maryland, he watched in disbelief as drops of wine appeared one after another at the bottom of a chalice when congregants continued to line up for the Precious Blood—even though the wine had run out when a young man "chug-a-lugged" all of it. "Every person who wanted to receive the Precious Blood was able to receive it," he noted with awe.

This goes to *Hebrews* 11:3, which informs us that "through faith we perceive that the worlds were created by the word of God, and that what is visible came into being through the invisible."

When we choose to serve Him—when we glory in God—anything can and does happen. He draws close and brings forth from nothingness. He created the universe from nothing. He multiplies what is necessary for us to serve and suddenly finances go our way or there are friends when we need friends. Things come out of the "blue." A crisis turns into a blessing and the Light of His love slices the darkness.

Adoring God brings a terrific force. He illuminates with shafts of light. Tapping into that brilliance is the key to many miracles.

Light is life and light is love.

Especially does it tap into healing. "Approximately one-third of the Gospel is taken up by the cures wrought by Jesus in the brief period of His public life," noted Father Raniero Cantalamessa, the preacher of the Pontifical Household in Rome. "It is impossible to eliminate these miracles, or to give them a natural explanation, without distorting the whole Gospel and making it incomprehensible."

17

When You Hit 'Rock Bottom'

Prayer affords the opportunity for the Holy Spirit to enlighten and work within us—and He does so in various ways that can be viewed as miraculous. Time and again I have seen miracles spring from faith (if that faith does not waver). We live in extraordinary times and should take advantage of the extraordinary graces.

When we suddenly see through the "fog" these are the shafts of God's illumination.

As the pontifical preacher warned, "the miracles of the Gospel present unmistakable characteristics. They were never carried out to astonish or extol the one working them. There are some today who allow themselves to be fascinated when listening to those who seem to have certain powers of levitation, of making things appear and disappear, and other such things," which tend toward the occult. Occult miracles are dangerous.

But they are outweighed by good ones, and those good ones come from the Light of Jesus Adored if we adore Him as the shepherds did.

All around us, it grows all the brighter when there is darkness.

A Muslim woman who was part of the king's inner circle in Morocco, but who was later jailed (after an attempted coup), detailed the incredible account of twenty years behind bars in the most hideous conditions imaginable—a detainment that ended with an intervention of the Blessed Mother.

It was in 1972 that Malika Oufkir, daughter of Moroccan General Muhammad Oufkir, was imprisoned with her mother and siblings after their father attempted to depose the reigning and brutal monarch. She and her family would not see freedom until 1991.

During her time in prison, Malika was to encounter an array of experiences terrible even by the standards of the gulag: isolation, freezing cold, and rotten food often contaminated by the feces and urine of rodents, when there was food at all. At night, Malika and her sisters lay terrified as swarms of flea-infested rats crawled over them.

Most of this occurred at an ancient desert "death camp" called Bir-Jdid in the southern part of Morocco. Officials wanted them to die for what her father, who was promptly executed, had done—and for many years the torment proceeded with unremitting cruelty, stealing their health, looks, and youth. Malika was but a girl of eighteen at the start of the ordeal.

But there were subtle signs of heaven's presence along the way. At the outset, before they were totally isolated, a local "prophet" foresaw that they would be detained a very long time, but that after a horrible ordeal they would be saved by something "miraculous."

After fifteen years of isolation—mostly in the intensely guarded prison of Bir-Jdid—the miracle came in the form of an extraordinary escape.

The Oufkirs were able to tunnel out of the prison using only a spoon, the handle of a knife, and the top of a sardine tin—then flee to a major city despite hot pursuit.

It is here that the Blessed Mother—known to Christians and Muslims alike, indeed famous for her appearance at Fatima, an Arabic name that means to "abstain" and some say "destiny"—comes in. While the Oufkirs were building the tunnel and concealing it every night, writes Malika, who was raised Muslim, "the guards carried out a painstaking inspection, even in the little room where the tunnel was. They beamed their torches into corners, they looked everywhere, under the beds, on the ceiling, in the cavities. They tapped the floor with their feet listening for a different sound, the faintest echo."

But incredibly, they never came upon the tunnel. The Oufkirs attributed such intervention to the Virgin, for whom they developed an intense devotion.

It was to save their lives.

"No guard ever set foot on our stone slabs. They walked round them, stopped just in front of them, and that was all. We were convinced the Virgin was protecting us: the first time we opened up the hole, the irregularity of the ground formed the shape of the cross, the length of the stone slabs. We made another cross out of cardboard, which we placed on top of the last layer of stone before sealing it up. We called the passage 'Mary's tunnel.'

"We believed this so fervently that we prayed on our knees when we opened it up every evening and when we closed it every morning," continued Malika. "We had rejected Islam, which had brought us nothing good, and opted for Catholicism instead. Mother, who had spent her childhood in a convent, knew all the prayers by heart and at our insistence taught them to us, although with reluctance [for she remained Muslim]."

But the children gravitated toward Christianity, and so "Marian" became these Muslims that one of the sisters, Mouna-Inan, changed her name to Maria. And during the 1987 escape, heaven intervened outside the prison gates as a pack of vicious, wild dogs threatened. "Their leader came forward baring his fangs, growled and looked poised to attack," recounted Malika in the book. "We froze, like statues, and held our breath, waiting for a miracle. Which, improbable as it seemed, was what occurred. The dog gave an unfathomable whine and slunk away, followed by the rest of the pack."

When they were recaptured, news of it spread around the world, and pressure on the reigning tyrant prevented their being tossed back into such abominable conditions. Instead, for the next five years, they were detained comfortably under house arrest. The escape was widely described as a "miracle." No one thought a human could get out of Bir-Jdid.

But they did. They did at the behest of Mary. It is documented in a riveting book.

At the police station, realizing they would be okay, and that a brother they worried about was alive, Malika almost fainted.

"Someone went to fetch me an orange juice," she said. "They opened the window and told me to breathe deeply. The police station overlooked a church. I looked out distractedly. That was when I saw her. Mary. The Virgin.

"Nestling in an alcove, she was holding the infant Jesus in her arms and gazing at me with a benevolent expression."

When you hit rock bottom, then you have located a foundation on which to build. This is where many blessings are! Can *you* think of tragedy that way?

Often, the biggest favor God does is to level the playing field.

God's a builder and sometimes that involves demolition. What He tears down is our evil, which can be in the way of our obsessions, our lusts, and especially our selfishness.

Most of the time when God has to clean house, it's because our pride has piled rubble around us.

We get blinded and we get "attached" to the rubble (there's that word again). We think it's concrete, when it is old cardboard. And we let it rise on all sides: ambition, over-competitiveness, things that always have an "I" in front of them.

In other cases, it's not so much that we have done anything wrong but that God is trying to clear the way for an expansion.

He wants to build something. He wants to bless us anew.

As John Paul once wrote, illumination comes from purgation.

So many times in life, we just can't seem to reach holiness without God sweeping everything aside. Major upheavals in our families, health, or careers are often enough to place things in a different perspective. It's amazing how quickly the world we hold so dear can disappear! When things collapse (jobs, education, bank accounts), we discover how fleeting they were to begin with.

It's God Who's always there—He is the only permanence—and what He is trying to show us is that we should cling to Him and that we will be restless until we rest on *His* foundation.

He never said life would be easy, just worth it!

Persistence and even joy in the face of trial (especially surrender to the Divine Will) paves the road to the miraculous.

"Anytime I have ever stressed about not having enough money to pay the bills, the situation gets worse," noted a woman named Julie who e-mailed me. "The more I try to control it, the less control I have. The very instant I give it all to God and bless and bless and bless the financial situation, however grim, the money flows in ways that truly do not seem physically possible."

Anytime God tears something down, He is giving us the opportunity to build something better.

See His Hand in everything and it is easier to put everything into those awesome Hands and with the flow of His Creation.

There is the mystery of suffering and yet let's think about it: when we have pain, when there is even a tragedy, it brings us to the greatest simplicity.

Suddenly, we have an entirely new perspective.

(Is this not one major explanation for suffering?)

The clutter of life is swept away by suffering.

It cleanses us. It makes our pleas to God more direct (and intense). It reduces pride, which is extremely important. It strips away pretense. It brings us to our essence (which is naked before the Lord, if truly we are before Him).

The same is true of tears.

What is crying? Why do we weep?

We see the supernatural link to suffering and cleansing, noting too, as I said, that in the majority of statue miracles, it is Mary *weeping*.

Is this sadness for the state of the world; a simple manifestation of the Holy Spirit (as in the gift of tears); or both?

Ordinary tears cleanse the eyes.

Tears of grace (and suffering) cleanse the spirit.

They are a fount. They soften. They are a purification. Noted an astute commentator on this very topic: "The Spirit allots to each one individually (as Paul said) just as the Spirit chooses. One of my spiritual mentors, a renowned Benedictine monk, had taught me that there were three rules for the Christian life:

- Don't fuss
- Love God
- Don't fuss

"I learned the second one by the age of nine when I heard my call to the priesthood and said 'Yes,'" he remarked. "The other two I am still learning!"

God gives everyone equal gifts, although such is rarely apparent to us. In the ways of the world, we esteem certain gifts more than others—those who speak publicly, for example, or are in Hollywood, or are government officials. Often we look around and think *everyone* has more blessings than we do—when in fact you have gifts as great as any.

This is important! You may be a receptionist, gifted with the ability to smile. Do you realize how important this is? (A "simple" smile may turn around a person's entire day—and lead to a chain reaction.)

Are you good at taking care of kids?

This is important to God.

Do you have the gift of generosity?

Or kindness?

Or patience?

Do you have the gift of humility, or mechanical ability, or uncomplaining housework?

Don't undersell yourself: what you do in your home may be of more significance to God than anything you see in the public arena. God loves the hidden and simple and if he has kept you that way, it is a sign of His favor or protective Grace. How strange it is that after two thousand years we still don't get this! Christ paid very little attention to the elite; He was with the common folk. Especially He was and is with those who love, which is the greatest gift of all.

If you can love, if you can smile, you are close to Him and a gifted person indeed.

When we love, we have access to the truth.

The more we love, the more clearly we see.

That clarity leads to healing because it isolates or names the problem. It's incredible how clear the air becomes when we name a stronghold (or should I say a stranglehold). Pray deeply until the Holy Spirit reveals what needs to be revealed and watch the negative leave. Be persistent! Keep the Name of Jesus on your lips! The same is true of stress. This can be caused by a lack of faith or by a root spirit of impatience. Impatience does not stand alone; it leads to many other negative emotions and robs us of tranquility.

Clear the spiritual air of your home by commanding out any negativity that may have entered. Do so, of course, in the Name of Jesus. Go deep and pray until you feel a real calm pervade your house. Employ blessed salt. Use Holy Water frequently. Ask a priest to bless your home. Make sure a Crucifix hangs in each room. When we pray from the heart and especially when we fast the bad drifts away like the smoke that it is.

Give yourself the greatest gift: that of being able to exude love like Christ and to find rest in His loving tranquil Spirit. Many tensions in our lives or other blocks are caused by spirits that are hovering in our midst but that in our hurry have escaped our notice. A spiritually clean home is a home devoid of tension, a home without strife, a home with no jealousy, a home where there is love, clear thinking—and good baking! It is a blessed home. Once we clear the air, it's remarkable how good everything seems.

18

When God is on the Scene, He leaves Nothing to Chance

Do you sometimes feel like you're hanging from a thread, that at any moment disaster could strike, that there are a million hazards out there and sooner or later one of them will get you? Are you afraid that genetic factors or exposure to carcinogens or the wrong diet is going to lead—inevitably—to cancer? Does every ache and pain cause fear? Do you figure that an accident of some sort, a breakdown, a heartbreak is just down the road?

It is not. Much bad does not have to be. We all die. There is redemptive suffering. But at most points in our lives all forms of the above can be prevented by closeness with the Lord.

He pervades all. There is no darkness in Him. Scripture tells us that. He is there for the intricate working of every cell in our bodies. And He can reverse damage and renew us both spiritually and physically. With Him there are blessings. Without Him, there's entropy; things fall apart. We tend to think of Him as Someone Who created everything and then has let that Creation spin off on its own.

That's not the way it is. The Lord is what vivifies us. He is throughout our beings. And He can affect anything in our systems—if we let Him (if we don't think life is mechanical, like a clock). God is our power and it's up to us to start thinking of Him that way. Begin seeing Him everywhere all the time, in the ordinary, in the extraordinary, and you now are under the control of a Being Who can reverse damage.

How's that for hope! And it's true: God is everywhere and does everything just as electricity powers all the motors in your home, without your seeing it. Have you noticed how subtle most of His miracles are? He will slightly inflect light. He will cause a candle to drip in just such a way that it could be seen as an angel (*could*—always leaving room for faith, and doubt). He will cause bark on a tree to grown in a fashion that resembles the Face of His Son.

These are His little miracles, and they extend to our own physicality. His slight touch causes our cells and tissues and organs to go in the right direction.

We all age and we all grow ill and the body will eventually break down, but we do not have to speed up the process. We are not destined for cancer. We are not destined for Alzheimer's. With faith, we are destined for the fullness of life. When the time comes when we need a doctor, we pray for God to come through the physician.

When God is on the scene—when He's in control, instead of just the doctors—we are no longer at the mercy of guesswork. The Bible says the weapons of spiritual warfare are not carnal but mighty in God. Let Him into every part of you. Let Him take over. Let Him permeate every cell.

Life is not a roulette wheel for those who invoke Him with faith, and that means realizing that there is not a single illness or handicap that He can't correct. There is nothing He can't do. He created and can suspend the physical laws.

What if that sharp pain in my arm is a symptom of a heart attack?

What if that pain in my abdomen is caused by an abdominal aneurism?

What if that flutter in my chest is a dangerous arrhythmia?

What if that occasional abdominal discomfort is a tumor?

We all go through this, and when we do we need to invoke the good Lord to take total control of circumstances.

He can halt anything bad. He can correct any situation. He will direct you if you need a physician. He can prevent illness from striking when we ask for that protection on a regular basis (praying preventively).

In prayer, if something feels really serious, naturally, we should take advantage of God's gift of the medical community. But it is time to stop surrendering to stress, the caprices of a mere physical viewpoint.

As pointed out in a book called *Stress Less* by a Christian doctor named Don Colbert, we bring many maladies upon ourselves. Stress is deadly. It's a vicious cycle.

"So many people today are far from experiencing 'perfect peace' because they do not trust God and their minds are not fixed on Him and His ability to protect them, provide for them, and guide them into every good path," writes Dr. Colbert. "They spend their days and nights worrying about the past or fretting about the future."

He gives countless ways of attacking stress—from what we eat to how we sleep, act, and pray—but the bottom line is always trusting in God.

"Anytime I see a patient whose health is deteriorating because life is spinning too fast, I explain to him that life is not a sprint, but a marathon," says the physician. "He or she needs to slow down and enjoy the slow jog through life. Those who race through their days at a breakneck speed are 'striving'—they are in hot pursuit of things temporal that they believe they personally must own, accomplish, or make happen."

Are you on a treadmill? Are you too "busy" to enjoy life? Is it affecting you?

"I'm afraid I'm going to lose my job . . ."

"I'm worried about my children . . ."

"I'm worried I won't be able to pay the bills . . ."

Get off the treadmill of stress—of fear—and know that God is everywhere that we let Him.

Is He too big to fit into your schedule? You really have to ask yourself that. It should be asked every morning. It should be asked through the day.

Is God in my schedule? Do I have time for Him?

When we're too rigid—when we have things set too firmly, when we have designed the day, without prayer—God is absent.

Due to free will, He lets us have our way.

The result is that we strain and scurry about and don't have enough time to do anything.

In many cases, the faster we work, the less we get done.

Do you set a schedule and adhere to it no matter what He may want to do? Is God in your schedule, or (as should be the case) is your schedule in Him? Are you willing to be spontaneous, or do you refuse to let God slip into your plans?

Remember, God often works through the unexpected. He works through spontaneity. He is always waiting for openings and those openings frequently occur in ways that we don't schedule; the key is making sure that we don't close those openings through blind determination (which leads us up a blind alley).

The more time you have for Him, the more time you have, period. The more we get done. And the better is our work. We are anointed. When we go with His flow, we live in a way that is "organic."

That's to say, when we live in God's Will we live in a way that moves gradually and powerfully and grows with the strength of a tree (not in the haste of a weed).

It may not seem perfect, it may not move at a breakneck pace, it may not expand in expected directions—but when we move with the Spirit of God we move with a potency that can weather the storms that prematurely bring old age.

We bear fruit.

Notice the way God works with plants. They grow best when they grow in the way He intends, completely in His Providence. Often, it's not the way we would have it. There is irregular growth. It may not seem "perfect." But it lasts because it is healthy. It is well rooted. It gets the job done. There is an enduring forest. What seemed like a long time was time well spent.

On the other hand, when we take over, when we try to force a plant to grow too quickly (for instance, through use of too much fertilizer), or try to make it too perfect (by over-clipping), we cause it to burn out because in our rush we have become creator.

Ambition is like fertilizer. Frenzy is phosphate. Perfectionism is acidic.

Turn disruptions into opportunities.

We have to live by certain strictures. We must be organized. Yes.

But we also have to be open—at every moment—to the Spirit. We have to realize that when God alters our plans, He may be preventing a circumstance that would have caused us harm we never did see.

When something comes along to disrupt your plans, go with it. Go with the flow. You'll find that God makes the time up to you. Let God be God!

He is creator and He wants to create your schedule.

If something comes up to disrupt your plans—if suddenly you have to go somewhere, or take someone to an unplanned stop—use that time wisely.

Use that time to pray.

Use that time to sprinkle blessed salt out your car window on the way to the errand to sanctify your neighborhood.

When you turn every tedium into an adventure, into a mission (for Him), into closeness, you open a door to blessedness.

To let God take over is to pray without ceasing and realize that even when we are doing something we don't want to—even when we are running out to do a chore when we had planned to be at a desk working—we can be in tune with the Lord if we turn every errand into a holy event.

Just letting go for an hour when you really had it in your plans to *work* that hour (or do whatever it was you were going to do) will open you to grace.

Offer up the frustration.

Yes, we have to have a certain time-table. Yes, we have to be at certain places at set times.

Just don't overdo it.

Let the Holy Spirit be with you when you plan your day and watch Him turn it into the most productive ever.

19

Don't Focus on the 'Itch' But on the Ointment (and Anointing)

Now let's look at another aspect: how God puts certain people into our paths as part of His Divine Plan, and how in other cases people put themselves into our paths in a way that sometimes contravenes that plan.

Each of us has an equal role in Creation and to fulfill what God has for our lives we have to *step into the blessing.*

That often means a clean break with those who are not supposed to be alongside us.

Folks who are not meant for us can greatly hold us back.

They can prevent us from realizing what God has in store for us. Sometimes, they can badly trip us up. The feeling of unsettlement is often the Spirit talking.

A problem this is! We don't want to hurt feelings (and should do everything possible not to). Moreover, we have to be careful not to persecute: often the devil would have us focus negatively on someone to attack that person.

Caution here.

(Always: mercy.)

But there are also folks who don't know their place and infringe on your zone of comfort and they should not be there. It is not that they are bad people. It is not that they aren't equal. It's that they simply are not where they should be. They don't know their place.

In some cases, there is evil. We must have a degree of separation from those who are living in darkness.

Perhaps we are meant to help such a person. We are always called to pray. But it doesn't mean that we have to expose ourselves to oppression.

We carry the spirit around those who are close to us, and so we can pick up spirits of jealousy, of infirmity, of anxiety, and so forth.

Feeling "drained" every time one has to speak with a person is a signal.

At the same time, we must have faith and know that God will put the *right* people in our paths. Follow the rule of prayer; pray about everyone.

Sometimes, we are led to them by unfortunate events. Something "bad" can happen and through the experience we run into someone who later turns out to help in a larger situation (a positive one!). They are what this preacher called "Barnabases": "While they were ministering to the Lord and fasting, the Holy Spirit said, 'Set apart for Me Barnabas and Saul for the work to which I have called them,'" we see in *Acts* 13:2.

Barnabas was *called* to work with Saul and it flowed miraculously.

Pray that you always know your "Barnabas" as you also pray for those from whom you may need more distance!

Now, another spiritual rule: unless absolutely necessary, don't engage with antagonists.

When provoked, step back and say to yourself (as many times as you need), "I don't have to get into a fight over that."

When we step back, we give God room to operate.

It's when we engage with someone or even talk about it, as I said, that the sting, the nettle, the venom, remains.

Talking about evil can give it power and when it does a curse finds germination.

When we ignore insult, it closes the door to infiltration.

One of the greatest tests of life thus is to turn the other cheek. If we love whoever insults us and return good for evil, harboring no ill will, the curse will not "alight" (to use the expression from *Proverbs*). When we release resentment, we're joining forces with the way He forgave on the Cross. As patiently we endure an irritation, the wound heals and the way to the miraculous widens.

One woman wrote about a husband who desperately needed a kidney transplant. A crisis this was, with no exit, it seemed. There was only one person who matched his blood type—a sister who was estranged.

They had a back and forth with her, and finally, to the horror of all, the sister announced that she had reached a decision and didn't want to donate the organ!

She wouldn't do it. And it was galling. It was devastating. Now, the woman's husband had only weeks to live.

But remarkably, instead of harboring bitterness, this man's wife stepped back, settled down to prayer, and through prayer came to her own remarkable decision: She would forgive the sister. No matter what, there would be love. Evil would not be returned for evil. She prepared a letter of forgiveness.

At the last minute, before the letter reached her, the sister changed her mind and offered her kidney against all expectation!

It's a mystery why we must suffer such tests until we see in it a path toward perfection. Difficulty punctures a hole in our pride and affords us the opportunity to love. Forgiveness is a manifestation of love projected outwardly.

God loves it when we can fly above a sorrow, disappointment, or insult and find His comfort; if you want Him to multiply what you need, send Him the ingredient of enthusiasm. Refuse to immerse yourself in setbacks. A widow of 9/11, Cheryl McGuinness, whose husband was the pilot of a plane that hit the Trade Center, says she wants other people to realize that no matter what disasters or pain occur in life ("no matter how horrific they can be"), those tragedies can be overcome by "having a foundation that we can draw on in times of tragedy."

That foundation is seeing the Hand of God in everything —which then makes it easier for us to put everything into His Hands. Let's repeat it: seeing the Hand of God in everything makes it easier to put everything in His Hands.

There is no situation from which He is absent.

And although it may look like it to us, He is never random.

Letting one's thoughts hover over an aggravation is counterproductive and must be stopped through discipline. That means controlling what you think. In your head is that constant inner dialogue and you have to make sure that it's devoid of anger. At the first negative thought, step back; halt it. Command it away. Do this every time it comes. Put it in Jesus' Hands. Soon, doing so will be easy.

Reverse the curse! Love those who despise you! This is "doing purgatory" here on earth indeed! Look at it as an opportunity to purify.

There is nothing that should gall you because there is nothing anyone has ever done that goes unseen by God and will not be addressed by Him in due course here or in the hereafter.

20

The More Enthusiastic We are Toward God, the More He Sends His Grace

Are you *joyful*? Can you find happiness even amid the most trying of circumstances?

A while back we visited with a friend whose wife had been diagnosed with breast cancer. They are in their forties, a bright young couple from a foreign nation with young children. They had everything going for them and then suddenly this had struck, bringing about that tortuous course of surgery, radiation treatments, and chemotherapy.

Their response? "Oh," said the husband, who is one of the most loving and spiritual people we have met, "this has been such a great experience! *It has brought us so close to God!*"

Instead of morbidity, he was bubbling with enthusiasm. Can you imagine responding to a crisis like that?

Much easier said than done, of course. It is the height of faith and it shows that with enthusiasm we find joy in anything.

It may take a while. We may have to strive for patience. We may have to pass through even more excruciating suffering.

But when we're enthusiastic, God never fails us.

Was Jesus always joyful? Was He always happy?

Well, He certainly didn't seem full of joy on Calvary, and all of us go through trials during which we can't or don't exhibit overt joy. During this life, we will always have sorrow as a companion.

But if we're enthusiastic toward God, if we have the faith that Christ had, we have that great inner peace (a form of joy) even in the most crucifying circumstances.

When we see life as a trial and suffering as an opportunity for advancement, even these become the source of enthusiasm (in the most daunting situations—though let us pray that we achieve this without such daunting circumstances).

Think of the Blessed Mother. She was devastated during her Son's Crucifixion; how could she not have been? But there's no record of her giving up. There's no record of her collapsing in grief. There is a record of her waiting with the disciples in the Upper Room with unbounded enthusiasm.

And that enthusiasm led to the descent of the Holy Spirit.

With prayer and praise we find gladness in every turn of life. This may sound difficult for those who are grieving, ill, out of work, or depressed, but it stands as a real challenge. In the Old Testament they greeted kings with song and dance and when we do the same—when we constantly thank God, when we find endless reasons to send Him joy— He alleviates sadness.

Viewed the right way, every crisis is an opportunity and every event has potentials that are both good and evil. It's up to us to spot the good in every crisis.

Mostly, we have to thank the Lord for what we normally take for granted.

When we focus on what we have as opposed to what we *want*, we develop enthusiasm for God and with this enthusiasm (and in proportion) comes His grace.

Our friend's wife? She's doing fine. She's through with her treatments and back to life with zest and at last report is looking perfectly normal—far better than anyone expected. Prayer! Praise! God loves those who find joy in every adversity and leads them to see a way out of every problem—even those that seem to have no exit.

Joy is our ticket through life. It's what we should strive for. It's difficult and sometimes just about impossible, but if we can approach every aggravation with a smile, if we find happiness in each struggle, if we transcend gloominess, we place shields around us.

Joy is the halo of brightness that plows through the darkness of life.

21

If You Want Real Happiness, Look Inward and Find the Hidden Power of Kindness

It is the harmony with God's laws that gives us purpose and joy. Upon clinical death, said a person who had a near-death experience, one of the first lessons was that "there is a reason for everything that happens, no matter how awful it appeared in the physical realm."

In Heaven, nothing on earth seems like such a big deal. Great suffering is little in terms of eternity. When we die, we'll say, "Of course!" or "I should have known!" as we review those things that were learning experiences (but at the time seemed like tragedies).

None of us wants to go through this. Hard to understand? Yes.

"It is always springtime in the heart that loves God," the Cure of Ars declared. I get this from the marvelous book, *A Bedside Book of Saints*. What were some names of the early Christian monasteries? "The Bright Place." "The Delights." "The Gate of Heaven." "The Happy Meadow."

"The soul of one who serves God," said St. John of the Cross, "always swims in joy, always keeps holiday, and is always in a mood for singing"!

"Laugh and grow strong," was a saying from St. Ignatius.

St. Teresa prayed to be delivered from "sour-faced saints."

The point? Joy heals. Joy sweeps away pessimism. Joy transcends the little trials we each encounter each week and sometimes every hour.

Joy calls your soul to heal your body, over which it rules. Even death should not daunt us. Look at how radiant John Paul II was right to the end! "The perfect love of God," said St. John of the Cross, "makes death welcome and most sweet to the soul." Joy also chases away evil.

Perfect love casts out fear and it is fear that so often robs us of gladness! Yet everything that happens does so for a purpose; God truly is in charge. He knows your smallest discomfort. He is everywhere.

Fighting evil? "They wage war on the devil as though they were amusing themselves," said Chrysostom of monks in his time. "*They have no sadness.*"

Joy is a measure of our generosity. And it makes life what it should be: a trial, yes, a fight against evil, but one with a supremely happy ending if we serve Christ, rising above the sorrow of this passing world with the love of God's delight.

If there is an issue or direction you need to discern in your life, one of the best measures is the amount of joy in what you love.

It may seem like an odd expression, but what we love does not necessarily bring us joy.

Many are those who "love" their money, their clothes, their cars, their homes, their luxuries, their "toys"—but such are more burdens than the cause of happiness.

You may love someone and not have joy in that love. If so, something has to be straightened out. The same is true with what you own, what you do, and where you are.

When you seek closeness to God and seek your true self, you are led to purity. To thine own self be true; if need be, turn your ship around; fix your marriage; distance from yourself hurts your self image. Be your true "you" whether that's "smaller" or "bigger" than what people expect. Let God guide and define you.

Too often, what we do in life—what we strive to love—doesn't bring us joy because we allow ourselves to be put into a box. We do what others have defined for us to do or what we have formulated based on the acceptance and judgment of others.

This is why there is a lack of joy, the fullness of which comes when we are who we really are and are doing what God had in mind for us to do, what He appointed for our joy, and when we look for rainbows instead of clouds.

Be who you are. We all have missions in life, and we lose our joy when we stray from those missions.

That mission may be "small": We may have been meant to work with a shovel instead of a computer, as a janitor instead of a salesman, as a teacher instead of an author. But God doesn't want us to do big things to glorify ourselves. He wants us to seek the big in the small.

We stray from our missions when we don't think they are "important enough" in the eyes of others—forgetting that the prestige of the world counts for nothing. We don't realize that great souls are placed at every "station of life," and that God has put everyone in roles through which they can serve Him and benefit others. An engineer—or a janitor—can be greater than a senator. A librarian may be a more mature soul than a famed evangelist. Seek God. The Lord is often revealed in what is quiet, and such is an ingredient of balance: to know who we are.

It's when we stray from our true vocations that we lose joy even though we may have a job we thought we would love. Your mission is your spiritual path. Don't let the world block it. Other times, we don't reach high enough. We stay in that box others have created for us and don't expand our lives because we're afraid of how others will react. That's tragic. We should never limit ourselves based on the judgments—or expectations—of others. Don't define yourself by the notions of others. Don't let them keep you down. When we move out of our box and into the realm of joy others will be activated into jealousy or feel threatened because they are challenged to follow. They are insecure because they are afraid we will change. We will have left *their* comfort zone. We may even estrange members of our family.

If it has been done in prayer, however, and grants peace in that prayer, we should go for it; we should seek out the full extent of our missions; we should realize our dreams (however big or "small" those dreams seem). We should ignore those of questionable motives. We should be who we are in the essence of goodness.

Don't let others drag you down. Don't make decisions based on guilt. Let God decide what your life is supposed to be, and you will find joy in everything.

22

God Wants You to Live a 'Large Life' and We Do That Through Him

Meanwhile, don't be the judge of others. Judgment kills.

We live at a time when it's very popular to criticize. Whether we turn on the radio, television, or listen to religious debates—within our own faith—the trend is to go after each other's throats and see who can hold most tightly for the longest period.

Many times, there is a rationalization (we can almost always rationalize the negative). We excoriate political leaders in the name of a moral issue (not just criticize them, but assault their very beings) and we criticize the Church— even attacking bishops—in the cause of "saving" Christianity. We shout at each other in the name of free speech.

When we die, we may be startled at how God looks at that.

We may find, for example, that it's more important to love and to forgive—to forget—than to genuflect on the correct knee.

Christ admonished *us* to cast the logs from our own eyes (before we go looking for blemishes in the eyes and lives of others; and how many of us heed Him? He was not legalistic. He had a different approach, He had an incredible message: that whenever we see something astray in another, we should keep quiet and first look inwardly.

In other words, as soon as we want to criticize, we should head right into prayerful introspection, cast out whatever may be in us (often we detest in others what we subconsciously detest in ourselves), and then pray for the other person.

A priest once said that when we die, we're going to discover that most people are better than we thought. When they're askew, they may be going through trials, enduring hardships, carrying unseen burdens.

That's not to excuse evil—nor to be naive. We need to discern evils. It is to say we should first think the best of others. There are few things worse than false first negative assumptions.

Do we have to admonish? At times, yes. But we should do that directly to the person, with gentleness, with respect.

Kindness is the keyword. It pleases God. It gives you the chance to be blessed anew. And it erases all those past negatives for which we will otherwise be held accountable in eternity.

"If you are earnestly conforming yourself to the image of Jesus Christ, sharpness, bitterness, and sarcasm disappear," wrote Father Lawrence G. Lovasik in a book called *The Hidden Power of Kindness*. "Kindness is our imitation of Divine Providence. Kindness adds sweetness to everything. It makes life's capabilities blossom and fills them with fragrance. *Kindness is like Divine grace.*"

When we die, Christ will immediately review our lives and how kind we were. It may well be the first thing He goes over—*how you made others feel.*

Kindness is encouraging others. It's making other people feel special. It's upholding the dignity of every human. It's enhancing dignity. It's making others feel important. It's being courteous. It's putting others first. It's being punctual. It's being generous. It's forgetting "self." It's smiling even when you don't want to smile (and then really feeling like it). It's surprising others with treats and compliments, even over little things. It's excusing others when what you want to do is criticize.

As Father Lovasik notes in his book, "delight in another's misfortune owes its origin to the devil, who, in the depths of his own misery, knows no other pleasure than that which he finds in our pain."

Do you want to be in consort with him? Do you want to imitate darkness and find fault with everyone around you? Or do you prefer the company of angels?

God loves a non-critical soul, and when we look inwardly we purify.

Go back and think of all the times you could have spent reviewing your own behavior instead of analyzing someone else's. Spend as much time looking at yourself as others and you won't have much negative to say about the others. Get in the habit of dispensing kindness, not spotting faults. Watch your joy mushroom!

"Kindness drives gloom and darkness from our souls and puts hope into fainting hearts," notes Father Lovasik. "It sweetens sorrow and lessens pain. It discovers unsuspected beauties of human character and calls forth a response from all that is best in souls.

"Kindness purifies, glorifies, and ennobles all that it touches. Kindness stops the torrent of angry passion, takes the sting from failure, and kindles courageous ambition."

Real power there.

True blessings.

There is also great power in stepping back and "knowing the other person's story."

I once heard the pastor of a local church talk about the time he wanted to approach one of the cantors and dissuade her from singing there any longer. She was a good person, very nice, but she had what could most charitably be described as a grating voice. There were those who complained, and he himself bit his lip every time she belted out the hymns.

One day this woman approached the priest and asked him over for dinner and he decided it was a golden opportunity to softly break the news that perhaps music was not her forte. He had to do something.

They had dinner and before he could approach her about the singing, this woman, a widow, described how she had been married to a good man, but one who had forbidden her from her great love: singing. He had not allowed her to sing anywhere near him, and perhaps nowhere, period. For years, she had to suppress the great pleasure she took in music. He had died, and while she mourned that loss, she also had experienced a tremendous sense of release because she was finally able to sing!

How could the pastor now say a word? How was he now to fire her as a cantor? He didn't. Now, he knew her story. (As it turned out, when the next pastor did fire her, there was such an outpouring of complaints from the congregation that he had to beg her to return.)

There once was a priest who said Mass frustratingly slowly but it later came out that when he spoke too fast, he had a stutter.

Do we take the time to "know the other person's story"? Do we really understand why those who bother us are the way that they are? Or are we quick to condemn without knowing very much in the way of detail?

When we do know detail, it tends towards understanding, which tends towards love. God knows the detail of every single aspect of our lives, and look at how much He loves!

Lent is a time for introspection and an opportunity to ask ourselves how often we cast a negative eye on others. When we're critical, we separate ourselves from God. It's when we give up the "self" and seek to serve and understand that we draw close to Him and experience the state of well-being He offers.

As the Bible says, the Lord gives peace to those who are in His favor; we are in His favor when we love.

Love, life, and light are not separate entities. They are one and the same. If we want one, we have to also seek the others.

One of the greatest enemies of grace is judgmentalism and rigidity. When we're rigid, we've created a shell. Grace bounces off. Think of how many ways you may be restricting yourself by being too rigid. Do you do everything your own way? Are you the only planner in your life (leaving out the Holy Spirit)? It's when we have pride and rigidity that we build a wall against the Holy Spirit—block blessings.

Years ago I drove the length of the Mississippi and was astonished to learn that many of its banks are now cement or earthen levees. Without those walls the Mississippi would inundate many homes—but at the same time the straight, rigid shorelines have prevented the river's overflow and rich silt deposits from nourishing surrounding farmlands. Instead, the soil shoots past the levees and is dumped by the rigid river into the Gulf of Mexico.

We do the same—we waste nutrients, spiritual nutri-ents—when we build walls around us. Such walls are formed by pride. When we think we know everything we need to know and can decide everything that's best for us with our own minds, with our own logic—without letting in God—we become rigid and "hard-headed" and even "hard of heart." This can also happen when we have not healed damaged emotions. Fears and hurts lead to the same kind of hardness, and once more the rigidity halts our progress. When we're that way, we lose our flexibility. And when something is inflexible it has an excellent chance of rupturing.

What's the solution?

Well, of course, humility. That's where we start. And forgiveness. That heals many emotions. And plain letting go. "Let go and let God" is the expression, and it's not just a cliché: Just about every day we're faced with a choice between doing things the way we think is best and doing things that are in the flow of the Holy Spirit.

When you have that choice, go with the Spirit. God wants us to be thinking and rational but He also wants us to be faithful and release things to Him.

Too often we set our minds on a plan or schedule and attempt to adhere to it so rigidly that we can't hear His small still voice within us. Often, God wants us to approach matters in a freer, more open manner—which means going with the flow and letting Him put things together.

I've seen this happen myself: where I'll have a rigid schedule during a trip or other endeavor, a master plan of how the day should be approached—with detailed plans that I have agonized over—and then I watch as those rigid plans yield little fruit.

On the other hand, when something unexpected comes up—and I'm open to it—it often leads to results that become much more productive.

The Lord opens up to us when we are open to Him and this is a lesson that can save us both time and turmoil. Much anxiety is caused by trying to hash everything ourselves—with our own rigid minds, instead of asking God to do it for us. By just releasing a schedule or plan, by just being open to an alteration, we invite the miraculous. Despite His size, all God needs is a little opening!

So make room. Look for His Mind more than your own. Let Him flow (like the mighty Mississippi once flowed) and watch all the fruit sprout around you.

Live a large life.
This is crucial.
You have to live big.
When you die, you want to have lived life to the fullest. With God, we accomplish that.
What does "living big" mean?
It doesn't mean fame. It doesn't mean being rich. It certainly doesn't mean getting fat. It doesn't mean a life so busy that it becomes a frenzy.
To live big is to live in the large faith of the Lord and that means to live without fear, which restrains us. To live large is to love.

It is to allow yourself to expand onto new territory and it's to see the small in the large and the large in the small; it's to be both secure and adventurous.

"Grant, O Lord, that I may know who I am and Who Thou art," prayed St. Augustine.

Faith equals living large while too often we limit ourselves and make our lives "smaller" due to anxiety. We don't travel because we're afraid of the plane and we don't move because we're afraid we won't be able "to make it" in a new place and we don't meet new people because we're afraid of their reaction to us. We don't try new things because we fear anything out of our routines.

And so we stifle ourselves unlike Christ Who roamed the countryside spreading good news to new places. To live a big life is to exercise our gifts fully and even to exercise gifts that we don't have.

How is that possible?

There was Maria Esperanza, the Venezuelan mystic. She wasn't known for music. But one time she prayed for a great song and came back with a musical praise to God that is one of the most powerful songs I have ever heard.

She prayed for the gift of music and *received* the gift of music (at least for the moment).

Some people are naturally cheerful. Do you have the gift of joy? If not, you can pray for it.

Do you have a good sense of humor? If not, pray to be funny.

Do you have the talent to cook? If not, pray for it.

The point is that we can pray for many gifts, although we may have to pray each time we want to exercise such a gift. Prayer makes life more full and varied and meaningful and larger.

When it comes to life, bigger (in the sense of doing all we can), is better. Of course, bigger could mean living in a tiny cloister!

Does that mean we should all pray to be preachers? No. Or writers? Of course not, as I discussed. God has a plan for our lives. We need to expand according to His direction, not selfish ambition.

The point is that we should live beyond the confines of routine, beyond the confines of tedium, beyond the restrictions of nervousness or fears or stereotypes that—once more—others cast upon us.

Step out with Christ Who showed that we could even follow his steps across the water if we prayed and if we believed in the miraculous.

Way too often, we let evil get the best of us. We allow negativity to prevail. We give it force. We feed it. That's because—as a preacher pointed out—we magnify darkness (illness, bad luck, accidents, family difficulties) instead of magnifying God.

Thus, a question: what do we place more faith in, the disease or the Person Who created the body (and, hence, can cure any illness)?

Magnify God. Praise Him. It is your great shield. See Him as larger than the Empire State Building (while the devil is smaller than that grain of sand, which is the way, in comparison, it really is).

A financial adviser shows you a red ledger. A child fails at school. There is a crisis in a relationship. A doctor comes in and announces: "terminal" cancer!

(Who on earth is not "terminal"?)

23

Darkness and Problems in Life Can Be Dispelled by Inner Cleansing

Don't "entertain" the negative or it will perform like a broken record and eat at you.

There will be no end.

Instead of a magnifying glass or microscope, instead of dwelling on every dark detail, use a telescope, looking at your problem through the wide end of it, so your problem appears small and distant.

Soon, that will be the reality.

God created everything. All is under His domain. And it is a great test of life to see if we can abandon our troubles and sufferings and ourselves to Him as Jesus did at Calvary. When we do, the Lord breathes our way. We ascend. Perhaps better put: His power intensifies around us.

We know a woman who had breast cancer that spread to the lymph nodes. She simply refused to accept the disease. She allowed a prudent measure of medical intervention and then blocked thoughts of the disease out—in effect convincing herself it did not exist. She has lived years beyond the expectations.

Don't let the evil one rob you of hope, don't let him reach into the purse of your blessings; when he does, he's robbing you of the chance to tap into the Power that created not just this planet but the universe. Unleash God's power, not the enemy's.

If you saw a tsunami coming, would you seek higher ground or dive into the murky waters to study it?

What we need to do is lift our eyes to the Lord and above the floodwaters.

Hit the high ground of Scripture.

Pull out the Bible every day.

Become consumed by His Word instead of the whisperings of evil.

And it does whisper—constantly! *You'll never be able to do that. You are going to fail. You'll be embarrassed. Why try? It's not for you. You can't be cured. You will die in agony.*

Baloney!

He is around every corner with a bat; he sticks out his foot every time he can. Yet we fall only when he diverts our attention. He can only defeat us if we play by his rules.

Look up, not down; look at the Crucifixion. Look at the way Jesus locked His Eyes on the Heavens before He died. The glory afterward!

Magnify the Lord, not illness, not hardship, not fear, not brokenness. Our Blessed Mother has said that with enough prayer, we will not even feel the passage into Heaven.

When we're diligent and disciplined without being mechanical, we find joy in the "current moment." Again: let the Holy Spirit flow.

"Joy of the moment" means finding happiness in every pursuit—laborious or not. It's enjoying what's on our plates now. It's not putting off happiness but often deciding to have it despite present circumstances. Savor the here and now!

Frequently, we put that off; we're too "b.u.s.y." (being under satan's yoke).

We're called to take life in smaller bites and nurture the personal side of life in an age of impersonalization.

Take life like that—one moment at a time—and you'll start to slow down and find much more joy on a regular basis. In this way, you'll also find it easier to love. Stop working yourself into a frenzy!

You'll also find joy with a clean spiritual slate. We are blocked from the enjoyment of taking life slowly by what you might call "little sins"—imperfections.

(Have you let little sins build up?)

This is more of a problem than we usually know. There are many "minor," venial sins—and while they don't stop us from receiving Communion (nor condemn us to the fires of gehenna), they can be enough to halt grace and require purification.

"God is able to make every grace abundant for you, so that in all things, always having all you need, you may have an abundance for every good work," it tells us in *Corinthians* (9:6-11).

The farther away we are from God, however, the less grace and the more "bad luck." We become blind to the joy available around us.

What is a "little sin"?

There are the small "white" lies.

Are you guilty of fudging, of exaggeration, of "fibbing"? A lie is a lie.

There is stealing.

When we gossip—when we're overly critical—we are taking joy from another or stealing from a reputation.

Do we look at what we do as closely as we look at others?

God wants self-regulation. He wants us to practice vigilance over our interior lives. When we don't, we fall into the sins of pride, covetousness, lust, anger, gluttony, envy, or sloth.

All these plug us up.

Make each day, each morning, each evening, an act of Confession. This will bring you the ability to live in the joy of the current moment.

What is sin and what is not?

"Bad thoughts, however filthy and abominable, are not sins," says a book called *The Seven Capital Sins*. "It is only by consenting to them that we commit sin. We shall never be overcome so long as we call on the holy Names of Jesus and Mary."

Realize this, act on it, watch each thought, and you'll be surprised at how free you become.

"There is nothing more difficult to cure than envy, nothing that causes the soul more suffering, vexation, and torment of mind," notes the book. "It gnaws at the heart like a worm. The chief remedies against it are fervent prayer, the practice of humility, and reflection on the grievousness of this sin, the difficulty of its cure, and the evils that flow from it.

"During the assaults of temptation, it is most useful to renew our resolution of suffering death rather than offend God; it is also good practice to sign ourselves repeatedly with the Sign of the Cross, and with Holy Water. It is of great help, too, to reveal the temptation to our confessor. But prayer is the best remedy of all, accompanied by cries for help to Jesus and Mary."

Otherwise, those small sins build like a dam that halt the flow of the living water which is the Holy Spirit. Inspiration can be yours, if you don't block it. Happiness is in your reach.

You are called to enjoy each moment—to live for now (not some distant dream)—and you do that by clearing the slate.

In school, teachers used to use erasers to remove chalk from the board and once a week a wet one to make it extra clean.

So it is with us. Often, joy is just a Confession away.

The cleanliness of the spirit is in direct proportion to contentment. When we purge those "little sins"—those things that aren't usually recognized sins—a whole new vista, a more peaceful vista, one of incredible Light, opens before us.

24

Lack of Joy Comes With Fear

Let's be clear. Lack of joy comes with fear. Do you fear so many things in life that you don't have a life? For some, that's a serious question.

At Mass a priest spoke about a woman he knew who was full of trepidation. She had a phobia about germs. Before she would visit friends, she'd call to see if anyone in the house (or coming to a party) had any sort of cold or other illness. She wouldn't let her kids eat lunch at school for fear of viruses or bacteria, and so would pick them up each lunchtime and take them home to feed them. When folks visited her house and touched the telephone, out would come the Lysol. And it wasn't just germs: she moved her bed from a window for fear an electrical line would fall through the glass electrifying her.

This is someone who not only didn't live life to the fullest but didn't live it at all. What she lived was not what God had for her. What she lived had been sent up by her flesh (or the devil). Indeed, one of Satan's greatest tools is fear (when we have fear we have faith in him).

That yields dark forces that feed energy into negativity.

Suddenly fears are realized.

It's a vicious cycle.

We imagine many dangers. While we are not to ignore real dangers, neither should we listen to those who peddle fear. "You are not to say, 'It is a conspiracy!' in regard to all that this people call a conspiracy, and you are not to fear what they fear or be in dread of it," says *Isaiah* 8:12.

There are all kinds of phobias. There are folks who won't leave their homes. There are people who scream at the sight of insects. There are those who have acute panic attacks over meeting new people.

We all have fear. Count me among those who are not thrilled with heights. And most are those who can't stand spiders—let alone snakes. The most common fear is death.

But I'm speaking about cases that are extreme.

The devil tries to obsess us with many things and we see this in habits and addictions. If you beat one addiction, he is ready to offer you another. Life is a constant smörgåsbord of potential obsessions. Only through diligent, constant prayer—and when we fast—do we feel truly free. (This is another reason why fasting is so potent.)

Fear is often the deepest part of us trying to nudge us into a truer sense of who we are. In Scripture, we are told time and again that the only fear we should have is of God—a clean fear that brings blessings.

"Though a host encamp against me, my heart will not fear; though war arise against me, in spite of this I shall be confident," says *Psalm* 27:3.

What do you fear? Who do you fear? How much time do you spend thinking about things that make you afraid, or at least anxious? Do you watch your internal dialogue? Are you mindful of what the saints called the "interior life"? "Peace I leave with you; My peace I give to you; not as the world gives do I give to you. Do not let your heart be troubled, nor let it be fearful," says *John* 14:27.

Sometimes, what you fear comes upon you. You can give it energy. And for sure you don't want to do that. "What the wicked fears will come upon him, but the desire of the righteous will be granted," says *Proverbs* 10:24, for fear is the opposite of faith. It brings "anti-blessings." It is obsessive, and obsession knows no bounds. "Do not fear, for I am with you; do not anxiously look about you, for I am your God. I will strengthen you, surely I will help you, surely I will uphold you with My righteous right hand," states *Isaiah* 41:10.

On TV, we see shows about those who are addicted to food, or celebrity, or objects that they hoard to the point where they live in squalor and can't even move. When we have pent-up fears, we have this clutter inside of us. In effect we have hoarded fears. We're stymied. We're blocked.

"So do not fear; you are more valuable than many sparrows," said Jesus (*Matthew* 10:31). Be bold. In prayer, step out. Knock down you affliction-addiction. Don't fear life. Live it. Live it to its fullest. Place all in the Hands of God. Your days will play out as they are meant to play out. With Him, all is good. There is nothing to fear, even death, when we are right in heart. Forsake the false terrors of the world. Cast out your various fears by name. Ask the Holy Spirit. He'll tell you how. The only thing we should fear, as a president once said, is fear itself.

Confession is a sacrament that emboldens us and purifies us and when we are clean, *un*clean spirits want far less to do with us. They don't fit. They can't meld with us. The use of Holy Water helps break their grip.

So does the Blessed Sacrament. It breaks fear. Those of you who live in large cities may know how when you turn on a light in the middle of the night, if you have cock-roaches, the bugs go scurrying around, fleeing for some-where to hide. The same is true with demons.

The Blessed Sacrament is a spiritual light. This is a real force and with it healings happen. Forces of fear and dark-ness hate the Light. And believe it: Adoration brings Light. "I try to go to Adoration on the first Saturday of every month," Stefanie Huguet of Moultrie, Georgia, wrote me. "One Advent, I was at Adoration and was praying the Rosary. It was a very bright sunny day and the sun actually hurt my eyes before Adoration. During Adoration and my private Rosary, I fixated on Jesus. I seem to do this often during Adoration, without realizing I have done this until afterward. Anyway, the Church began to fill with light, except the light seemed to be like fog. I could almost touch it but I couldn't. *It was the brightest light I have ever seen.* I felt a sense of peace that I still cannot describe. When I finished the Rosary, I closed my eyes and the light seemed to penetrate and get bright enough to go through my eyelids. The brightness was unbelievable! When it faded, I realized that I had been weeping throughout, but there was no pain or discomfort. When I left, the sun was still out and it was between noon and one and the day seemed very dull even though there were no clouds in the sky. It was like the sunlight was 'dirty' compared to the Light I saw in the church."

Prayer and trust dispel fear. Added Daniel Flies: "I have to share an experience that recently happened to my girl-friend and me. On August 8, 2009, we were watching *America's Most Wanted*. It was a very warm and muggy evening. All of the sudden the tornado warning sirens were going off, and we quickly turned the channel to find out what was going on, as of that point the show we were watching hadn't flashed an alert. Immediately we were informed that there was a tornado spotted in a city just a few miles away and it was headed toward Plymouth, Minnesota—where I live in.

"We quickly went outside and walked around to take a look. The sky was greenish tint in one direction and had a very dark, almost black wall cloud just to the west. We went back in to gather things and turn out lights. We quickly went to move my girlfriend's vehicle in the garage and she noticed a rotation in the clouds that were what seemed like just blocks away, as if they were boiling and spinning. Quickly we got into my vehicle and drove off; my first concern was who's with Jesus, as I live a mile away from a Blessed Sacrament Chapel. My instinct took me towards the church, and no sooner than being about one to two blocks from my home, there was this downdraft of sudden and intense wind. Debris was flying through the air and hitting my car, the vehicle was shaking, yet I just continued to drive towards the church. Finally clearing this very quick brush with the intense winds and making it to the chapel, we found that our Lord was not alone and there were people there. We breathed a sigh of relief and sat in the parking lot listening to the radio for the storm reports. Not long after things seemed to clear a bit more, we drove back down the same road in my neighborhood, only to find major devastation. There were news crews, power companies, and people everywhere surveying the damage. The very next day it was confirmed that it was an actual tornado touchdown. Forty-three houses damaged, trees uprooted, power lines were down and all thanks be to God, no one was injured. What I have come to realize is that we actually drove through the tornado. We were on our way to make sure the Lord was protected, when He was already right there protecting us. We were blessed with His great love and that of His mother's promise to those who pray the Rosary daily, and wear the Brown Scapular. After reflection on this whole experience, I felt it necessary to share this miracle and this story of our Lord's great love for us. I personally have been blessed by His Mercy and Protection in my life because I trust in Him!"

Jesus, I trust in You. With Him there are all kinds of miracles. There are huge miracles—healings, rescues. There are times when miracles are so awesome that folks simply don't believe it. Then there are the "little miracles"—the miracles that are hard to describe, that come as a sequence, the kind you have to "be there" to appreciate.

Whichever you are about to receive (and God has a reservoir for every one of us), we open ourselves best for them when we pray, empty ourselves, work at eliminating all selfishness, and let God fill us.

Make room for God, and He will come on a daily basis—and you will feel the "Hand of the Lord."

The Hand of the Lord is the biblical term for God's power in the lives of His people (see *Joshua* 4:24 and *Isaiah* 59:1). "Little children, believe that by simple prayer miracles can be worked," said a message from the Blessed Mother. "Through your prayer you open your heart to God and He works miracles in your life." Think of yourself as a bucket. If it is full of yourself—of your own motives, of your own ambitions, of your ego, and of your lusts—how much grace can God fit in? Even if there were room: is He going to inject nectar into muddy water?

This is where "emptying" comes in. Emptying is getting rid of sin but it is also letting in God. It's stepping out in faith. It's doing everything for Him and allowing His power to flow. When we seek that, we're hungering for the Lord, and according to Scripture, "He pulls down princes from their thrones" and "routs the proud of heart" at the same time that "He fills the hungry with good things"—with miracles (*Luke* 1:51-53). As it says in that same passage, it is then that He shows "the power of His arm."

The Lord desires us to follow Him in as strong a fashion as possible, and that means learning to toss away those things—objects, ambitions, habits—that get in the way. When we empty ourselves, He reaches down for us. Tragic as it might sound, the Hand of the Lord is seldom asked for. We just don't think to do it. In this life (the darkness of existence here on earth), it's hard to step out with the kind of unselfishness that God requires. Yet when we do that and ask for the power of His Hand with the same innocent faith as the early Church—when we confess our sins, empty ourselves, and purify—we open a treasure trove of miracles. It seems counterintuitive, but the "emptier" we are of ego, the less room there is for fear!

We can judge if we are empty or full of self by asking a few simple questions.

Do we think of ourselves first?

Do we look at every situation from our own perspective?

Is our first question how something will affect us?

Or do we look at everything from the point of view of others?

When we do the latter—every day, in all circumstances of life—our prayers cause constant wonders.

Call them the "little miracles," prayers for everyday things, but prayers that are swiftly answered.

In Acts, the phenomenal success of the early Church was attributed to exactly this. And we can tap into it too. We are faithful and empty—that is, available for Christ—when we just turn it over to God. Turn it over. Say, "Father, please do this in me. It's too big. I can't do it alone!" Let Him speak for you. Let Him act. The result will be those "little miracles"—and even healings: ones that aren't so little.

25

The Sensation of Tranquility Means the Spirit is in Balance and Healing Can Begin

The body and spirit are far more closely connected than we usually realize. What goes on in the spirit directly affects us in many ways. Usually we think of the two as distinctly separate, but the connection is completely intertwined. And it is the spirit that transcends and directs the physical. More simply put: all of the brain is in the mind but not all of the mind (spirit) is in the brain.

So it is that if there are defects, shortcomings, or taints in the spirit, these can physically materialize. They can manifest in the body from a spiritual force. Hard of heart? Maybe that can add to arteriosclerosis. Tense of mind? Perhaps that adds to hypertension. The day will come when we realize that many diseases, even cancer, can originate preternaturally.

This is not to say that *all* such illness have a spiritual base (chemicals, genes, and germs can make us sick through sheer physical etiology), but it *is* to say that a spiritual blotch, a taint of mind—or the presence of evil—often leads to illness.

Your spirit flows in and around you—organizes your physicality—and thus it is a healing of this spirit that often must precede a physical remedy.

When we are *not* healed in the spirit—when blocks remain—so are there blocks to healing. The physical is a reflection of the spiritual. Such blockages may be due to emotional disorders, occult contamination, sin we have not purged, or something we have failed to forgive. Unforgiveness causes many illnesses—as do jealousy, hatred, and anxiety.

We develop blocks in our spirits and through prayer must remove them. As one famous healing priest noted, "Most of us are aware of the necessity of prayer and Scripture for a good healthy spiritual life. Those who break these spiritual laws suffer." That's because prayer gives us harmony and balance, which are felt in peace, and when we are tranquil our spirits are affecting us positively. Scripture tells us that God grants serenity to those in His favor and that favor includes healing. A pure, balanced spirit is your best bet against cancer, heart problems, diabetes, allergies, infections, arthritis, and innumerable ailments. The spirit bolsters your immune system. He also heals our wounds. It is the Holy Spirit Who informs us as to what we need nutritionally.

The body is far too complex for us to understand, and medical information is often contradictory. First we are told that something is good for us (milk, cheese, meat, eggs, coffee, wine, vitamins) and then that it is not so good and then that it is good again. We don't fully understand the human body (perhaps never will) and to complicate matters, every body is different.

The only One Who can fully understand is the Holy Spirit—and the only source that fully knows *your* body is the soul (linked to the Spirit) that directs it.

So it is that when we pray we need to ask what we should eat or even how we should lose weight and the Spirit (through our minds) will answer. Don't get me wrong: No one lives forever. There are also crosses in life. But often we bring ailments upon ourselves and have to deal with them at a spiritual level.

The Holy Spirit will instruct you on what supplements or dietary changes you need and will also bring you toward balance. Health equals balance which is harmony with God Who is health itself!

If we have been exposed to evil, this evil, in whatever way it came to us, must be purged before it can manifest as illness. Remember: Christ often cast out demons before he healed a person. These spirits attach to us through the occult, illicit sex, anger, and other sin. Goodness and prayer, on the other hand, are "antibiotics." They cleanse. They give us peace. And this (the sensation of tranquility, which means the spirit is in balance) is when true healing begins. For that balance it's necessary to remain positive and one of the most astonishing lessons of life is that there is never a good reason to stay depressed. Depression is one of the darknesses that can transmit physically.

That statement may even anger you! Yet it's true: if we live the lives of saints (and I myself am not claiming to that), we rise above sorrow. We experience it, yes: all of yes go through sorrow. We grieve. But it should not cling to us. It can make us sick ("unblessed").

When we stop meditating on the underside of dark clouds and instead fly to the sun (Son) above, into the realm of the Great Physician, nothing can defeat us.

Literally, there is always a light at the end of the tunnel.

Does that mean if we get depressed we are not good? Does it mean we can never be down? Do the doldrums mean we're not pure?

Of course not. Everyone goes through it at various points in life and perhaps at many points. Depression can be a suffering, and suffering redemptive. Who is to judge? In some cases it even has a root in biochemistry.

The problem comes when we allow that pessimism to cling to us.

The keys are faith, love, and ridding ourselves of "self." Self is an anchor to the muck, and we don't need that! Meantime, love shields us, smoothing over conflicts, or eradicating the source of antagonism, while faith erases fear, which is the cause of much depression and illness to begin with.

Once we erase fear, we have peace, which brings joy. There you have a formula!

A state of Godliness is one in which joy from peace can be felt in the most bitter moments.

Christ raises us up while the devil depresses. When you recognize from whence negativity comes, often you are free of it.

We live forever and when we realize that true fact—really know it, every waking moment—nothing should get us down for very long. One day we'll look back and see that the "worst" thing that happened to us was but a learning experience.

Thus, every "bad" event is an opportunity.

Often, depression comes because we are "hung up" on something or someone or on ourselves. When we become morbid, it is frequently because we are too immersed in our "selves."

If our love is simple and pure, it will be without inordinate affection.

Now, does this mean we never get down? Does this mean we never grieve?

Again, it seems in life like we must know sorrow before joyfulness. There is pain. There is even tragedy. We never know what will happen. Our fear is that it will be something beyond that which we can endure.

And yet there's no such thing.

God never gives us more than we can handle. He tells us that in the Bible!

And those who have had mystical insights agree with the saints that every difficulty in life is a gift to be utilized in the progression of spirit.

"Why are you consumed with vain sorrow?" asked the Lord of Thomas á Kempis in his classic *The Imitation of Christ*. "Why are you weary with superfluous cares? Stand ready to do My Will, and you will find nothing to hurt or hinder you."

We also avoid depression—and larger problems—by buffering ourselves.

In prayer, tap into the foreknowledge of God. There you will find prevention.

Such is all relevant because it's important to pray before it's too late. You know what I mean: when you're hit with a sudden crisis, at first you feel overwhelmed. There's the feeling that you're in a hole and it will take forever to dig out.

Avoid it to begin with. Often, we can be relieved of an unpleasant experience and perhaps avoid it if we *pray about what we should pray about*—and "cover all bases" before problems occur. In other words, pray for the foreknowledge of God and His protection.

In meditation, heart-to-heart with Him, meditate on every area of potential concern and pray about each of those areas.

As you run down a list of possible problems, God will open up knowledge of what else may need prayer. Things will pop into your head. The longer you pray, the more precognitive you will become.

In prayer, we are led by the Holy Spirit.

This doesn't mean that you will never be hit by surprise. Life is full of them. Life is a test. But you will be buffered. Don't just wing a prayer. Pray about situations until there is a feeling of settlement. This is when prayers have been absorbed, when they have pierced the clouds.

Pray about hidden things—about the unpleasant and unexpected—and you will have that buffer; you will tap into His foreknowledge. Plead His Blood. Don't accept the negativity of others. This includes doctors. Too often we are told "bad" medical news and accept it instead of buffering against it.

Aim high. Pray without ceasing. Each day ask the Lord what it is you most need to pray about and watch as the pieces fall into place and a wall of protection rises before the enemy.

26

'Reverse the Curse' and Quench the Fiery Darts by Praying for Tour Antagonists

Emulate Joseph. Emulate Mary. Follow them and find the deep wellspring of the Lord gushing inside your spirit (and around you)!

Who am I, Lord? Let me live my life as the one You made. Form me according to Your Will—only Your Will, Lord!

Never, ever, mind what others think of you.

Go through each day wondering only what *God* thinks of you—not your neighbors, not your beautician, not the competitor—and your life will blossom like a flower that reaches upward blooming always.

Discipline leads to prayer and prayer leads to discipline and forms a joyful cycle instead of a vicious one.

Fasting is a great way to start and begins by teaching us to control our eating (one of the more difficult things we can do), which then translates to many other forms of orderliness. When we have discipline, we learn even to control our words and thoughts. We develop a way of rejecting bad thoughts and keeping only those that are good.

With this, God's grace flows; we have only to note how disciplined Jesus was.

Look at your emotions as wild animals that need to be tamed and note that only discipline will tame them.

That kind of order puts a bubble around us and does so by allowing us to detach from emotions.

Now, what about when we are cursed?

Curses do exist and to pray for someone who is doing us harm takes discipline because we don't want to! It doesn't seem "normal." Perhaps such is the definition of discipline: doing something that the "flesh" doesn't want us to do.

But it is the way out of a curse and the results are miraculous. When we pray for our antagonists we "reverse the curse." The bubble of prayer takes us (physically *and* mentally) beyond their reach. Jesus prayed for His tormentors and rose above them.

Most difficult is jealousy. All of us have envy thrown at us. It's very painful. It robs us of peace. It is a form of hate. When someone is jealous, they are wishing you a form of harm, and this is a negative "prayer" that can have ramifications. As *Proverbs* says, wrath may be cruel—but who can stand before jealousy?

And yet, we are not defenseless. Our defense is love. Our secret is discipline. When we repay animosity with prayer, the curse loses its hold on us.

Have you ever tried that, disciplining yourself not to think negatively about someone you dislike and praying for those who despise you?

It's hard. It takes practice. But it leads to a life of peace. It grants us order in our lives. A priest we know recently noted that "it is difficult to feel the peace of God unless one has first resolved seriously to be faithful to one's spouse, to pardon those who have offended one, to live by one's own work, to discipline one's instincts and desires."

If there is someone who is really bothering you (whose very name causes emotions to well in you, who even tempts you toward hatred), pray for that person (from the heart) and those emotions will fade.

Meanwhile, many are those who come to me with problems that involve evil. I'm speaking about both generic evil and problems caused by actual evil spirits. It is a time, in the words of the Virgin, when the devil is "unchained," and he has caused problems for all of us—jealousies, anger, problems at work, anxiety, depression, confusion, divisions in our families. His special hallmark is a combination of anxiety and perplexity.

In some cases his presence is clearly discernible, while at other times he comes with great stealth, without our knowing that it's him. He darkens us. He does so to entire societies. He tempts us to sin. On September 11 there was not just a physical darkness from the smoke at the World Trade Center but also a shroud of confusion.

By meditating on Christ's Blood, by pleading it, by washing ourselves in it, we banish evil. It's what defeated him—drop by drop—at Calvary. It's the Blood that flowed into every part of the Savior's body, and what was shed for the salvation of the whole world. It is the holiness of the soil of Israel!

And the most powerful way we can invoke the precious Blood is during Mass. Bring your problems to church. Bring your fears. Bring the afflictions the devil causes and *break* them during Consecration. When the priest raises that chalice, or when you drink from the cup, *there* is your opportunity to banish evil. There is your chance to dispel problems or habits or attacks that haunt you. There is your chance to get in all your needs.

Adore the Blood and invoke it and cover yourselves in the power that breaks all bonds and dispels all confusion.

Every drop is more potent than anything the evil demons can conjure. They can do *nothing* in the face of it.

Plead it all day. Plead it at the first sign of evil. If you have evil in your lives—if you're hurt, or confused, or perplexed, or frightened, or sick, or fatigued-- take these matters to the Eucharist and dispel them. Plead that the Blood of Christ washes all evil from you and you'll find that bondages are broken and light shines and a curtain of darkness and spiritual blindness is lifted.

This is why blood is seen in Eucharistic miracles—to remind us of what's behind the Eucharist (a power that transcends the entire universe).

Don't let people contaminate you. Forget about being offended. Forgive always and you'll find freedom. Don't drink the poison. As soon as you do, the enemy has you.

Have you noticed that when you accept an insult or even something that wasn't meant as an insult but that bothered you it pollutes your day?

It's like dye: a single drop can fog or discolor a bucket of water.

It's also like a weed: When we let the seed of a dandelion take root, it's difficult to get rid of—but when we immediately brush away that seed, it has no time to take root.

The same is true with how others treat us. It's always better to believe the best about another and excuse a slight, for it may be unintentional or just the product of someone's personality. Whatever the case, the important rule is that love sees beyond insults. It covers over faults. It transcends aggravation.

The test of life is responding to everything with patience. Whew! Again, easier said than done. Perhaps the key spiritual rule here—again—is stepping back. Anytime we are met by a challenge—especially something that seeks to provoke us—the wise thing is to take a step back, remain as aloof as possible from immediate emotion, and consign it all to the Holy Spirit. Pray until you have proper distance.

It doesn't come naturally. It's something we have to pray for. "Stepping back" is discipline, and discipline is the key to many spiritual challenges. Discipline yourself not to react automatically. Pray for that and it will happen.

Tough? Yes. When we get aggravated we want to give people a piece of our minds. And sometimes they deserve it! But when we do so we hurt ourselves—whereas forgiveness, immediate forgiveness, brings us contentment. All it takes is a little poison to ruin your day, so decide not to let that happen.

Christ will help you. He will justify you. In God's own time, justice will be served.

In the meantime, keep the stream pure. We heard a preacher admonish this: Don't drink the tainted water that the enemy sends. He wants to lure you into aggravation. He wants to taint you. Aggravate *him*. Laugh at him. Reject negativity. When you do that, the enemy flees.

27

Being Negative Stops the Flow While the Positive Taps into a 'Stream of Miracles'

Did you ever notice how when a negative person enters a room the entire dynamic changes? Or when we speak negatively? Something happens when we're suddenly pointing out the bad in every subject and picking apart everyone.

Observe the aftereffects: it actually influences the atmosphere of the room.

It's one thing to point out problems. We can do that (and often *need* to do that) with love and gentleness. It's another thing to be negative, which is a lack of love—and bears spiritual repercussions. When we wish something well, it flourishes, while a negative thought darkens the landscape.

Negativity gathers clouds. It collects a storm. *What is lightning but a large negative charge?*

Think of it as plus and minus. Plus gives. Plus has energy. Plus looks like a cross.

Negative, on the other hand, is missing the upright (is incomplete, a minus) and vacuums goodness out of us.

It especially vacuums away grace. This happens because when we're negative we distance ourselves from what might be called the "stream of life."

Society has grown cold. People don't treat each other so well any more. This seems in keeping with the passage in Scripture that says as evildoing rises, so does coldness of heart.

"From road rage in the morning commute to high decibel cell-phone conversations that ruin dinner out, men and women behaving badly has become the hallmark of a hurry-up world," notes ABC, reporting on a new survey that found nearly seventy percent questioned felt people are ruder than they were twenty or thirty years ago.

Have we not all noticed this? Have we not noticed the cars that cut us off, the folks who rush to be ahead of us in line, the way we can no longer get an actual human being on the telephone?

Our society has grown cold, and in addition to the effects of technology (which has numbed us), the cause can be traced to self-importance (a hyper-ambition that leads us to live in a way that is selfish and self-absorbed). "A demand for instant gratification has strained common courtesies to the breaking point," notes the report.

Rush rush. Do it now. Give it to me immediately. This is one crisis. The other is simple "unlove." We have become self-seekers. The result is inner turmoil and outward frenzy. And the solution starts with slowing down.

Half the reason for our rudeness and harried lifestyle is that we try to do too much. We pack too much into a day. We bite off more than we can digest in that quest to "get ahead"—to get ahead at work, to get to the head of the line. We all need to draw a deep breath and do what the Bible says: take one day at a time. Or we run right past blessings.

If this is happening to you, if you feel harried and on a treadmill, ask the Holy Spirit to direct the pace of your life. *Begin each morning with prayer* and plan your day during that prayer. Don't put too many things in those twenty-four hours. Be more realistic. It's when you start to build a long list that the anxiety and tension mount, which are then projected outwardly. Let God set your pace.

Many suffer from hypertension, which can also cause "adhedonia"—an inability to experience joy. This may be an actual spirit that needs to be cast out. During prayer, *cast away the spirit of hypertension* in the Name of Jesus and eventually it will leave along with its offshoots of anger, impatience, spitefulness, and sometimes outright hostility. Fill the void left by hypertension with patience. When people are rude to you, when they are cold, don't respond in kind. *Respond to ice with nice.* The ruder people are, the nicer you should be.

The void created when hypertension is booted out should be filled with love that connects you with other people.

This will cause you to glean the best in others. It will let you compliment them. If you go through life winging off compliments (right and left!), this will not only rub off but place a shield of warmth around you.

Nice is love. It is also humble. And here we have the key to cushioning ourselves from evil. When it comes to love and humility, the devil can stand neither!

Love shields us in a rude world and sparks a light in the darkness.

Love and humility defeat rudeness. They overwhelm it! When we *don't* react to insult, God takes over and rights the wrong.

Life is a series of tests, and above all, these tests revolve around love. We hear this constantly from those who have "near-death" experiences: When they return, they tell us that what Jesus wanted most to discuss about their lives was how often and how much they had loved. Think of this. He showed them how they emotionally affected every single person whom they had ever encountered.

Do you realize how good a compliment makes a person feel? How it lights something up in them—something they will pass along?

We must love in all circumstances—and must learn to consider each temptation to anger as instead an opportunity. Don't let rudeness bother you!

There is the shield of love and the opportunity to transcend the world and draw down special grace every time someone cuts in front of you.

We have to be especially careful of what we say. When we're close to relatives and friends, our tongues can give us a lot of trouble. In fact, most of our holiday troubles are caused by what we say. "Death and life are in the power of the tongue," says Proverbs—and when we look back at our lives, we see how powerful and sometimes devastatingly true those words are.

"The moment I understood how powerful our words can be, I repented for the wrong use of my tongue and asked the Holy Spirit to take control of it," says a Catholic author named Maria Vadia, who writes on this subject. "We can use our tongues to bless or to curse, to encourage or discourage, to edify or tear down, to bring healing or destruction. With our tongues we grumble, complain, criticize, gossip, slander and pass judgment on others. Our words are packed with power for good or evil, and basically what we say is what we get."

The best thing about being right, when you are right, is that you can be quiet about it. You don't have to say a thing. The truth lets itself be known. Remember this in the discourses of life.

Arguing rarely solves anything, and stokes the power of the enemy.

God will send events to defend you.

Are there times we have to be firm?

Of course. There are times we have to let others know they have hurt us. There are times we have to warn. There are times we have to admonish, especially those who are younger.

Silence is not always golden.

But often—most often, in the midst of turmoil—we don't regret what we have not said.

Talking is a plague of our time. Everyone talks—at home, on the phone, in the car, on the phone in the car, at work, on the computer (or even on "talk radio").

To talk to the extent we do opens us to evil because it is hard to talk that long without entering into criticality, pretension, or gossip.

"He who guards his mouth and tongue," says *Proverbs* (21:23) "guards his soul from troubles."

Often, we wish we could take words (or tone of voice) back. Strife occurs. We say what we wish we hadn't. Why keep going through this? The tongue is a fire that can consume us, Scripture also says—"a sharp sword," in the words of *Psalm* 57:4.

Remember that the most powerful night in history was a silent one.

When we restrain our words and emotions in the midst of temptation we graduate to a level that brings grace. We are not to use the "silent treatment" as a flog (which is a form of malice). We're to forgive and inform and move on.

The right silence clears the air.

It lets us see the other side.

It invites prayer.

Loudly proclaim the dangers of today, yes; loudly admonish evil; loudly warn when there is the presence of the demonic.

But discipline yourself not to react to everything.

"If anyone thinks himself to be religious, and yet does not bridle his tongue but deceives his own heart, this man's religion is worthless," says *James* (1:26 and 3:6). "The tongue is a fire, the very world of iniquity; the tongue is set among our members as that which defiles the entire body, and sets on fire the course of our life, and is set on fire by hell."

When antagonistic thoughts enter your mind, say, "Jesus, think this for me."

"Jesus, think that thought . . ."

"Jesus, control my tongue!"

To be possessed by Jesus is the only good possession.

As author Maria Vadia points our, our tongues are like the thermometers of our souls. They reveal the need to transform. Did you ever notice how negative words seem to draw down a pall of darkness? That's because there is actual darkness, says the author. "Grumbling, complaining, murmuring, and negativity are a sure way to attract evil spirits into our lives, and they come to "steal, kill, and destroy" God's blessings and promises from us," she notes in a book called *There's Power in Your Tongue*, quoting *John* 10:10. "When we use our tongue for evil, what is manifested in our lives is death, not life. When we grumble, complain, and confess negativity, we are really confessing what the devil wants us to say; we are confessing his 'report.' And those are words that produce death, not life."

This operates in surprising ways.

Vadia gives herself as an example.

She describes how in the 1990s, she was trying to sell a house. The "negative report" came from realtors who told her the market in Florida was slow and she might not be able to sell it. It was taking many months for others to move their homes, they warned. But Vadia rejected that notion,

Michael Harold Brown

pled the Blood of Jesus on her property—and, like Joshua, marched around her property in prayer seven times.

The house sold within two and a half weeks.

How many times in our own lives do we let the enemy program us for failure? The state of our hearts is revealed in what we accept as a true report as well as in what we speak, which tells volumes about the power of words. Especially we must be careful about angry ones. "Anger is one of the doorways through which the enemy comes in," says Maria. "This is another reason why we shouldn't stay angry or nurse our anger. Anger is an invitation for demonic activity. If you stay angry long enough, you're giving the devil an opportunity to 'steal, kill, and destroy' in your life."

In other words: when we get angry, we cause more harm to ourselves than to the targets of our wrath. Anger runs in some family trees and should be broken in the Name of Jesus. Those are unhealthy soul-ties. We get bound in such ties when we retaliate, lack forgiveness, and open our mouths. "The way we use our tongues is crucial!" Vadia emphasizes. "Remember *James*' word that our tongues are like a bit in a horse's mouth and like the rudder of a ship; depending on how we use it we will or will not make it to our destiny."

Negative thoughts and words often come from misperceptions.

We go through life with a vision that's imperfect. Sometimes it is *more* imperfect than at other times. Sometimes, it's distorted, as through a prism. Sometimes, we're outright blind.

And the reason is that truth is seen in proportion to our purity, our goodness, and our honesty. Do you see what is really there? Do you see the truth, the full truth, and nothing but? Are you sure there are not distortions in what you

136

observe—even things imagined, to which you are ready to react?

Sin after sin pile up to block us. We imagine that someone doesn't like us. We imagine they are talking behind our backs. We imagine they have done all kinds of things they may not have done. We fret about what will happen to us.

Before you criticize, before you argue, clear the logs in your eyes. Logs pile up and jam a river. It's also like a spring: clear water allows us to see the bottom (and the fullness of a creek) while water that's murky can hide what is in it (did you every notice where alligators live?).

The truth is clear only when the soul is pure, and so purify and see like you have never seen.

On the other hand, when we have purified—when we're clear, when we're humble—we get the living waters from Heaven. St. Teresa of Avila once said that the light of Heaven is like "a very clear stream, in a bed of crystal, reflecting the sun's rays," while Sister Lucia of Fatima described the angel she saw as "whiter than snow, transparent as crystal when the sun shines through it."

It is with that light that purity sees.

Look at the Infant. Look at His chaste father Joseph. Look at the immaculate mother. They will help you purify. They will help you see. They had the foresight of the Holy Spirit.

The eye is the window of the soul and impurities cloud it. We see worries that we really don't have to worry about. We argue with members of the family when there really is not much over which to contend. This happens especially at Christmas (when the devil is so active).

If we lie, or cheat—if there is deception in us—our vision is limited in proportion to our deception (or negativity). The same is true if we lack love. Love brings the clearest waters; it exits our mouths in kindness.

Good water is clear and bad water is murky from pollution or algae or some other imbalance.

In the maintenance of a pool is the need for the right chlorine, and the right filter that keeps the water from obscuring what we can see, the right pH.

So too in our lives.

This is why we must remove the "log" to see what we really can see. How often we argue on partial perceptions!

The answer is living and thinking and talking rightly. The answer is in being a blessing to everyone. The answer is in rising above the tugs of worldliness through purity. Resolve to cause everyone around you to feel better. Give everyone a blessed day. Watch your interior life (every thought). Do you know how it is when you have a day where everything goes right—when all seems to flow with grace? Pray that everyone you come across has that experience. *Give everyone the gift of a day's blessing.*

This will elevate you. This will purify. Christmas is a terrific time to purify! Make it the gift to God next holiday.

And see like you have never seen before—all the way to Bethlehem.

28

Ask for Bigger Miracles

When we are purified, we are better situated for miracles.

How do we make miracles happen? With belief. Trust. That's how we get answers to prayers. We need to open up. The sky is the limit. God hears us—and responds when it's in His will.

It's up to us to better appreciate how much God wants to help us and even bless us specially. Too often, we limit ourselves. Too often, we pray as if we're confined in a closet. While that's a good place to go for privacy, we're not supposed to spiritually confine ourselves, and most often we do. We set limits. We believe only to a point. We restrain the blessings God may have in store for us.

We need to think big. We need to open up. Do not limit what God can do for you. When we're working for Jesus, when we're seeking to do His will, He will bless us specially, He'll help us accomplish the impossible, He'll expand our territory—often in a way that's miraculous.

So too is this true in our daily struggles. There is no point in allowing yourself to be oppressed by daily life and there is every need to rise above it.

When you have problems, when you feel down, you need to pray as if you *know* you will be heard and (if it's correct in the larger picture only the Lord can see), God will grant it.

Don't be afraid to ask (*John* 16:24). Ask beyond what you normally expect. God loves our requests. (It honors Him.) He loves to bless. But we have to ask and all of us should do that every day: ask for better and bigger blessings and better and bigger ways of serving and living His glory here on earth and then forever.

Did you ever notice that our God is a God of the last minute? That's to say, He often intervenes a minute *after* the last moment—when we think matters are beyond hope. The message: never give up!

Consider those with near-death experiences. There are many cases where folks were considered beyond hope and even clinically dead and then were brought back because so many prayed for them.

They describe going through a tunnel to a light but then being told (often by Jesus, sometimes by a deceased relative, or an angel) that they must return, and when they do, they note relatives praying around the "deathbed."

After tasting Heaven, many aren't too happy about that!

But the point: God can be a God of the very last moment because He sees all and knows all and controls all including time itself. He can slow things down. He can speed them up. He can accomplish creation of a universe in an instant (never mind the rescue of a human). With faith in God, we are never without hope, or beyond any time limit.

We have so many cases of severe cancer that disappeared after the patients were sent home to die and even a politician in the Philippines who had a severe case of AIDS from a blood transfusion—and yet now, after countless brushes with death—crisis after crisis—has no trace of the virus.

There was the case of a fellow from Florida who doctors thought had "died" during surgery. He was placed in a room where they put cadavers but suddenly came back to consciousness in the presence of a mysterious woman who then vanished.

Oh, those mysterious strangers! Oh, those last-minute rescues. Michele Bottesi of Rochester Hills, Michigan, wrote to tell me how "two times in the summer of 2003 I was called to visit the tomb of Father Solanus Casey [who has been declared "venerable"] at St. Bonaventure in Detroit. During the first visit my sister suggested that we touch our scapulars to Father Solanus's tomb, and we did. During the second visit a week later I felt a strong impulse to purchase a woman's scapular (white cord) in the gift shop, but did not when unable to think of anyone specific who was in need of one. Shortly thereafter, God placed me at the scene of a terrible accident in which a young man on a motorcycle was hit by an SUV on Rochester Road (five lanes of fast road) and critically injured. The fact that the man was not hit by a second car was in itself a miracle, as he was thrown vertically across several lanes of the road. The scene was horrifying, but I felt compelled by God to get out of the car, approach the man whose broken body was convulsing terribly on the road, remove my scapular, and place it on him. In doing so, I realized that the scapular was a man's scapular (brown cord); God's plan at St. Bonaventure was for me to buy a replacement scapular because He had plans for the one she was wearing. Very awesome. For some reason this young man was given this pivotal intervention by God and Father Solanus, so he would have a scapular as his life hung in the balance. I felt compelled to remain until the paramedics were notified that the scapular was to remain with the young man. A man with completely gray hair who was dressed as a priest (black clothes, white collar) appeared on the scene just after the young man received the scapular. I only remember saying to him, 'Thank Heaven that you are here!' At no time did he approach the injured man, who was just feet away from us. He was amazingly calm and did not seem worried about the young man's condition. He seemed so peaceful. After we spoke I did not see him again. After instructing the paramedics about the scapular I felt Divine permission to leave the scene and all the way home felt the immense presence of the Divine Will of God in all that had just taken place: total consolation which superseded any worry for the man despite his horrible condition. That heavenly consolation lingered for about two months. Two points seem to stand out from this event: the scapular is a sacramental from God. And the second? God wants us to unite ourselves to His Divine Will and trust in Him always, despite how tragic events appear to us."

And how late in the game it seems.

29

When Problems Won't Go, Head for the 'Light' and Let Shadows Fall behind; God Can Heal Your Past

We live at a time when spirits are manifesting in an unusual manner. It's a time in which the veil is thinning. The good news is that we're seeing more supernatural manifestations than in memory. Even the mainstream media—which used to all but totally ignore spiritual phenomena—are covering it. There are miracles. There are angels. There are insights into the spiritual realm. Heaven is touching the earth.

That's the good news.

The bad is that Satan is likewise energized. Spirits of good and evil are extremely active and protection is essential (especially of our young). So is cleansing.

"Just about every parent I talk to has experienced some if not all of these attacks within their own families, mine included, which is a constant battle," said a reader who cited the harassment of children before Sunday Mass. Are there misfortunes in your life? Are there strange tensions? Does anxiety predominate? Is there too much illness? Is there sudden, inexplicable antagonism?

Evil comes at us many ways, including from misunderstandings and resentment. Good people can be a conduit for it. All it takes is a little "crack" for the smoke to enter.

Like wood, we are only as strong as our weakest points and so we want to uniformly strengthen ourselves.

Sometimes, spirits afflict folks with runs of bad "luck" that are incredible.

"I wonder at times if my family and I have been cursed, since we've had a horrendous string of misfortunes," wrote a woman who has been in touch with us for years. "Here are some of the things that have happened in under four years: I was hospitalized with pneumonia two weeks ago and can't get well. The week before that, we were burglarized and lost over $7,000 worth of goods. Several months before that, our family car was destroyed in a freak accident while sitting in a parking space when another car went airborne and plowed into it. Both of our daughters' cars have been badly damaged by deer running into them. One daughter was seriously injured by being hit by another driver. A few months before *that*, our family business was nearly destroyed by a chain store moving in across the street and our income was greatly reduced. My husband was diagnosed with emphysema. He also has had several heart attacks which permanently and seriously damaged his heart. Our vacation home burned to the ground after being hit by lightning. One of our daughters became addicted to drugs. I was diagnosed with a brain tumor.

"I go to Mass and Confession," she continued, "and try to follow our Catholic faith, and I've been active in converting others.

"But I just feel like I must be doing something terribly wrong for all of these things to have happened to us in the last three-and-a-half years. I just don't know what. This string of problems is starting to affect my faith. Please help!"

My advice to her: start by asking the Holy Spirit to guide you. Petition Him and wait until you feel His peace. Then implore Him to send you the Spirit of Truth. Ask specifically for that spirit so that root causes are revealed to you. Pray until you feel a great love for God. Do this especially during Communion. Love is your shield and illumination.

It is the Light toward which you must head.

Once you feel you have done that enough, begin allowing your thoughts during the Rosary or Eucharist or Adoration to cast out whatever spirits come to mind. Be specific: *spirit of infirmity, spirit of anger, spirit of anxiety, or even spirit of lung disorders, spirits of coronary disturbance.* Pray about each one casting each out until you feel a sense of power and peace. Ask the Holy Spirit how the controlling spirit was allowed such jurisdiction (there may be some hidden, or generational, spirit), and break any bondage by simply and powerfully declaring that you break these things in the Name of Jesus.

Do this very strongly and powerfully several times a day, while using Holy Water and going to Mass, and it will work wonders (in God's time).

Remember what can bind you—making you prone to evil: lust, anger, and attachment to the material.

Clean your house with Holy Water and then seal it.

"We are instructed in *Matthew* 12:43-45 that when the home is 'empty, swept clean, and put in order,' the evil spirit 'goes and brings back with itself seven other spirits more evil than itself' and 'the last condition of that person is worse than the first,'" a viewer of *Spirit Daily* reminded me. "We understand this to indicate the need after 'cleaning house' to call upon the Holy Spirit to fill all those voids with the Holy Spirit."

To fill yourself with Christ means Scripture on your lips along with the Name Jesus.

Many times we have problems that we don't recognize. This leads to everything from little anxieties to traumatic accidents. However it comes, shake it off; gravitate to Jesus. This brings us—and everything that haunts us—into the Light. Train your eyes on Him, not your problems. Move straight forward. Never step in reverse!

Don't focus on what evil has done but how it is *un*done.

Head for His Light and the shadow of your burdens will fall behind you.

Now, what about our pasts? What about what has haunted us before? Can God change time?

What if you could go back and remedy certain things in your past?

In *2 Kings* 20 we see that God can even reverse the movement of shadows. "Said Hezekiah: 'It is easy for the shadow to decline ten steps; no, but let the shadow turn backward ten steps.' Isaiah the prophet cried to the Lord, and He brought the shadow on the stairway back ten steps by which it had gone down on the stairway of Ahaz."

And so going back in time is easy work for God and He can correct past mistakes for you. He will right the wrongs you have done—if He sees a devout, repentant, prayerful heart.

What a promise.

Take advantage of it.

This is not to say we actually relive the moment—not on earth. We don't go through a time warp. There's no Rod Serling. There's no flying by the stars (not while we're in the flesh).

But yes:

God can reverse harm we've done or shortcomings and can re-present the opportunities we missed—perhaps in a different way, but with the same effect.

He can restore lost opportunities.

Let go of needing something, advised one person, and it will unfold for you.

Cling to nothing but Jesus.

He can go back in your life and rearrange everything *if you are truly repentant, if you have confessed;* especially *if you ask in faith.* This brings a taste of Heaven to earth.

Are there children you would have liked to have had a closer relationship with? He can now cause you to be so close that it makes up for past distance. Is there a friend you ended up not being friends with? Spiritually, He can rejoin you. Is there a task you should have achieved? He can grant another opportunity that bears identical prospects (in ways you could never anticipate).

In prayer, go back and meditate on the situations and ask God to remedy them. Send love where you had not sent love. Soothe past feelings. Forgive, forgive, and forgive again. In eternity, you will see it the way it should have been and even here will reap the benefits.

Ask God to go back and restore lost moments. Spiritual failings? He can greatly increase your development—in such a way that the failure no longer serves as a negative. A career miscue? He can recover whatever you think went down the drain.

When we die, there is a period of self-discovery during which the social masks we wore on earth dissolve and the true self is revealed. Make your true self heavenly. Get a vision of your future and head for that.

If you did things that were unhealthy, *ask God to go back and heal your body* from the abuse (or neglect); He knows no bounds. All is *now* and in that flow is the Power of His Hand.

Promise God your love, give Him your faith, forgive those who have wronged you—and He will make up whatever you need made up. There are no efforts you ever made (except for selfish evil ones) that were wasted.

In Heaven there is forward and backward and in prayer we can do that even now in forgiveness. In Heaven, we remember our real identities.

Let there be no self motive. Extinguish all greed. Let selfishness be unknown to you. Act out of pure goodness.

Fight the good fight and the Lord will "reverse the curse" (and *course*) of the past and you will attract grace like a magnet!

Actions done solely out of love for Him are spiritual dynamite (whereas vanity is like striving after the wind).

All we need to know is in Scripture.

"The Bible resonated with truth as I had been given it," said a man, Dr. Howard Storm, who had an afterlife revelation. "After weeks it dawned on me that I was not the first person to discover the Bible and find the truth. God speaks directly to us through the testimony of men and women written thousands of years ago. The more I read the Bible the more enthusiastic I became. There are frequent times when you are reading the Bible that the Spirit of God speaks directly to you. You shout inside, *'Yes! Yes! Yes!'* It is like discovering a magnificent jewel."

It can also be like discovering a life preserver.

It is always a blessing.

"When I read the Bible slowly, prayerfully, openly, it was like having a conversation with God," continued Storm. "It was, and still is, as if the words were alive. They resonated with vitality and excitement in my mind, as if I was engaged in a conversation with the Divine.

"This was surprising since I had tried to read the Bible on a few occasions in the past, and I had found it dry, lifeless, and confusing. The difference was how I approached it.

"If you sincerely ask the Bible to speak to you, and read slowly, listening to every word, it speaks to your mind and becomes alive in your imagination. The more you allow it to speak, the more vivid it becomes."

Indeed. Pray. Read. Listen. Let God speak where He does loudest: in the deep silence of a trusting heart, and if you want a special life blessing, endeavor to read the entire Bible.

30

Clean Your Deepest Self and Find the God of Surprise

You are now building a buffer around you. Here's another step:

When folks throw garbage at you, treat it as just that: a case where they have been trashed themselves and are looking for an outlet.

Don't take it personally. Bless them and move on. Life is ten percent what you make it and ninety percent how you take it.

They call that the "law of the garbage truck." What it takes, sometimes, are "buttons." First, a reset button, like on your computer. Every day, ask God for the contrition and grace you need and then reset your spirit to forget the guilt and anger and resentment that have built like trash from past events; start the day like it's a clean slate.

Each morning, "reboot." Clear the screen. See Christ. *Don't remain mired in your personal history.*

How many past insults, past hurts, past missed opportunities or antagonisms or "failures" (or sins) still haunt you? Did you ever consider how often you let them weigh you down just by thinking of them?

Let nothing negative enter. Put up a "no vacancy" sign. When people try to feed you their garbage, when they say hurtful things, treat it like a foreign language.

Stop marching to the beat of the enemy.

When you open the blinds on a window, it is to let in the sun (not clouds). Look at your mind the same way.

When we think about something over and again—an insult, a wrong action by someone, a misconception—we only bind ourselves to that person, and we surely do not want to do that. It rots us from within.

Forgive, reject the scraps, and move on without looking back. Burn the trash. (Don't become a landfill!)

"Oh Lord," we must say, "protect my mind from wrongful thoughts, and from the hurts of the enemy. Seal me." Force the negative out *(No Vacancy)*.

Learn to quickly replace negative thoughts with positive ones, worries with hopes, "downer" thoughts with thoughts about things you plan to do (that are pleasant) and it can change your life and perhaps your afterlife, for when we die we step into the reality to which we are oriented.

Use the right "software." Reboot. Have discipline. Control your thinking. Flash on the sign. Fill yourself with the Word of God—all the "rooms" of your inner sanctuary— such that no evil will enter.

God may be ready to surprise you.

Are you ready?

Are you prepared to receive this?

Have you "cleared the way"?

Miracles await you—always. Never mind if you are "down and out." Never mind if you feel like you are last in line. God can make the "last" to be first *by simply shifting the direction of the wind!*

When He does, the landscape changes. Hasn't that happened at times in your life? Suddenly, events form to rearrange your very existence.

Don't be afraid to let that happen. Often we don't receive what we could *because we're not ready for it.* We have blocks. There are obstacles. There is emotional or spiritual "woundedness."

It is time for you to clear them. It is time for you to go back in your life and ask for healing.

Remember that God takes blocks in your life and turns them into steppingstones.

Feel stuck? He will "unstick" you. Stalled? He will "unstall" you. Hopeless? Have hope. For God can easily—mightily—get you where you need to go in ways you would not have thought possible.

Through our choices, we choose to partake of His blessing—His surprises—or wallow in inertia (which can become quicksand). What God wants is for you to climb from the muck and move ahead. When that's done, anything is possible.

Here's the catch: the Lord wants to see you advance in love. He wants you to think kindly of everyone. This is the "preparation" for surprise. He wants you to view everyone as part of the same Plan.

We possess love only when we allow it to enter.

Recover your destiny. Make sure you are on track to fulfill your mission. How often do we think of this—and realize that no matter how astray we have gone, Christ can get us back?

Recover your destiny. That's important because according to the research I've done for an upcoming book, one of the first thing that will be "reviewed" when we die is how much of our missions we fulfilled. We want to see those completed!

In prayer—invoking the Holy Spirit—you can find guidance in what your mission is (and how to fulfill it). The idea of a mission is one of a number of consistencies you find in near-death experiences.

There are others:

—Those who have "died" and return report that the experience was unexpectedly pleasant. It was not fearful, in most cases.

—Often, the first spirits they encounter are deceased loved ones, their guardian angels, or Jesus.

—They see how "little" things can be extremely important.

—They see that love and how they treated others was paramount.

—They perceive an incredibly beautiful landscape.

—They feel an absolute sense of peace and well-being such as goes beyond any earthly description.

—They see everything in their lives as if it is a movie.

If you feel you have fallen short, ask the Holy Spirit to erase past failures and open up vistas that will recover your destiny (and your authentic self).

Prayer to Redeem Lost Time *(Saint Teresa of Avila)*:

O my God! Source of all mercy! I acknowledge Your sovereign power. While recalling the wasted years that are past, I believe that You, Lord, can in an instant turn this loss to gain. Miserable as I am, yet I firmly believe that You can do all things. Please restore to me the time lost, giving me Your grace, both now and in the future, that I may appear before You in "wedding garments."

Amen.

31

Refrain from Resenting Anyone

How many are bound to their pasts? How many still think too much of things, events, and people in their personal histories? How many have not fully moved on to full joy (which means purgation)?

This is why we call on God to cleanse our personal experiences. You may recall the saying that "those who forget history are condemned to repeat it." One could add that those who hold onto history for too long are bound to repeat whatever they are holding onto.

It's one thing to learn from a past mistake (that's what the old saying says to do)—but quite another to hover and obsess over past unpleasant experiences.

When we do that, when we always return to our past—and especially when it was an emotional "trauma" (such as a broken relationship)—we have baggage. We have blindness. We carry *cinderblocks*. We look backward and stumble forward. This is unhealthy. It's also dangerous. Please take note that our hearts go where our thoughts are—and we don't want that to be a place of darkness!

Have you held on to something that negatively affected you? Are you stuck in a past dispute or rejection (replaying it over and over? Do you have hurts from a relationship, from children, from a friend who "did you wrong"? From a boss, a co-worker, a neighbor?

If so—if you are sending emotions into the past—you're maintaining a "negative soul tie." You are giving it energy. Whatever bad encounter you had has been kept alive. You are bound to precisely the negativity that hurt you—allowing it to replay like a broken record (which will both waste your time and drive you to distraction).

Each time you think of something negative in your past, you are reigniting it. And this has effects you probably don't imagine. There is actual power in thoughts—great mysterious energy—and when we die we will see the results.

Each time there's a negative memory it's like putting a cinder block in a canoe.

Pretty soon, it's very tough going—and tougher still to keep the canoe from capsizing. The same is true with the deceased: Many people can't go beyond grief. Hovering for too long over a dead relative or friend can hold a soul from properly "moving on" or spark a disturbance in the realm of unseen souls around us. It turns love (and the wonderful expectation of reuniting again one day) into morbidity.

We live on average for forty-one million minutes. How many of those minutes and hours do you want to spend on the negative?

When we send negativity, or tap into it, it returns like a boomerang.

What binds blinds. Do we want to keep our eyes and minds on the past and enter eternity backwards?

Look ahead, straight. Look up. Aim for the "higher reaches." This is your destiny. Joy awaits no matter what has occurred, if you tap into it.

When we look at the past with love instead of resentment, the Force of God comes through us to those to whom we are sending thoughts of forgiveness, of reconciliation. That power heals, erases, and cleanses.

Bind yourself only to Christ. When we are bound to Him we are *un*bound from evil. We are bound to the openness of time. "My yoke is easy," He said. "My burden light."

Imagine meeting up with every person you have known in Heaven. How do you want to feel when you do? Do you want to have to explain a grudge?

Go back through your personal history and let the Holy Spirit show you what you haven't yet released. In prayer, meditate over past injuries, forgive whoever may have caused those injuries, pray for the person (or persons), feel God heal you, and do your best to send love—deeply and with sincerity.

Remember: many of those who hurt you may have had a false impression of you, and you of them—which led to conflict. Often, when we think the worst of someone, it's because we *want* to. When we're angry, it is often rooted in pride. Sometimes, it's the defensive part of us. Pride declares the truth as an insult.

If you can feel love flow, peace will follow. So will blessings.

Get in the rhythm of that and your blackboard will clear and like an untethered balloon you are ready now for the ascent upward.

Are you about to burst? Do you feel tensions well up, beyond what you think you can contain at times?

It is a cycle we all encounter:

The growing, *the swelling*—and then the bursting point.

We are seeing this occur with the economy and we see it also in our own lives.

Pop. Suddenly, it's gone. There is relief. There is release. Suddenly, the Lord comes to the rescue. Sometimes, we're not happy about the way that "pop" comes. It seems bad. It is for our good. It can be through illness. It can be through trauma. It can be through accidents—or close calls. It can be through losing a job. It can be painful. But it is the Lord saving us from ourselves in ways we don't always understand.

In many cases, we swell because we *have held onto something*. Often God deals with our swollen selves by pricking the balloon we too often become.

Pride goes before the fall.

"Nor do people put new wine into old wineskins," says *Matthew* 9:17, "otherwise the wineskins burst, and the wine pours out and the wineskins are ruined; but they put new wine into fresh wineskins, and both are preserved."

Is there negativity welling inside of you? Are you swollen? What has become too big for your "skin" to contain?

It is a matter of free will but then comes the bursting point and the Lord with a scalpel. Call it spiritual appendicitis.

What is causing your tensions to inflate? What in your life is about to rupture? What is beginning to grow that could reach a crisis point?

Breathe the Holy Spirit in and out, let nothing else build within you (but love), and if you are going to "burst," burst forth with a grace that will transform you and everything around you. Let *that* be the only thing that collects in your spirit!

Let it be the only thing you exhale.

In such a way can we begin to live Heaven from this earth.

If you want joy, look for the accents in your life. Look for the subtle ways that God communicates. Look for the ways He is guiding you.

God is a subtle Sovereign. He pushes nothing down our throats, except, at times, when matters reach crisis level. He is not usually brazen with His miracles.

Instead, His miracles come by *accenting* what is there before us in our lives, among our loved ones, and especially in nature.

He uses others to nudge us. He sets something before us. He limns the horizon with coincidence: you spot a special flower; a rose is especially red; there is an unusual sunset; the sun rises and a beam of its light falls right on you; what you cook has a special little touch that gives it unusual flavor; events move smoothly—nearly seamlessly; there is a gentle rain that seems to speak to you; a bird peeps at a particular moment; in an hour of angst you pray and the clouds slowly part.

God speaks through nature but does so in a way that does not flare like neon nor do anything to infringe upon our choices, which would compromise the tests of life.

In the realm of "signs," many are the photographs that are just *slightly* inexplicable—not enough to declare as miracles, but a communication to those who are in tune with the Spirit.

The same is true of answers to prayers: many healings have that edge of the supernatural, but can not be proven as such.

The Lord prefers anonymity! He is too humble to take credit. But He does not leave us alone. Look at the tides—how just a slight nuance of the gravity from the moon moves entire oceanic systems. The ocean shifts in a way that is barely perceptible but in the course of an hour or two alters the very shore—contracts a beach, revealing hidden things.

There are also the tides in our lives: one day the waves are favorable, the next they are not; one day everything goes our way; we'd like to bottle it; we'd like to repeat it at will.

But we cannot. We go through favors one day and tests the next. As the tide goes out, sometimes it is favorable; it grants more sand. Other times, it can create dangerous currents. Every time, it varies according to location and time.

Fall and rise, rise and fall. These are the vicissitudes of life.

When we accept them, we enjoy even the challenges; we fear not the currents; we "ride the waves"; we transcend them.

What has He sent to you of late? What is the pattern of His "small" consolations in your life? What has God accented for you?

Meditate on them and you will find answers.

We enjoy each little accent or prompting that directs us, or consoles us, or simply gives us joy.

Free yourself by ridding yourself of doubt.

It is in this way that we bear good fruit.

"By their fruits you will know them," said Jesus—and there has always been the question: what did He mean by "fruits"? We ask because it's such an intriguing statement—with the potential for evaluating matters we otherwise can not judge.

"By their fruits."

A fruit is something we produce. It's nutritious. It's something that thus helps others. It's pleasant. It's delectable. It comes from deep within. It depends on the roots. We can say and promise many things—we can talk—but actions (and what we actually *produce*) speak louder than words. At the supermarket, they even call it the "produce" section!

Our fruits also identify us. "For the tree is known by its fruit," states *Matthew* 12:33. Are we good "fruit inspectors"?

Now meditate on *that*: we know a tree is an *apple* tree because of the apples, and that a *peach* tree is a peach tree because of its peaches, and a fig, and so forth. We know there is something wrong if the fruit from a tree is cracked or tiny or bitter when it should not be bitter. What fruits are people around you producing? What are your own fruits? What if a tree produces *nothing*? We know what Christ did to the unproductive fig, which was consuming resources—taking—but yielding nothing. When that happens—when there is no fruit—we don't know the tree. We can't identify it. It is someone stuck in the past. When we do not produce "fruit," we can't recognize ourselves!

Is what is coming from you building people up—nourishing them—or doing the opposite?

Do we suck all the oxygen out of a room?

Do we edify or drain energy?

By their fruits you can judge how much sunlight is in a person's life and how well rooted they are. Stay in the company of those who produce righteously; leave in the past those who offer poison.

Fruit is produced not for the tree alone but to nourish fellow living creatures; they also serve the purpose of reproduction, for fruits carry seeds. This is a main purpose. The fruits of our society have turned bad because we have cut off fruit that bears perpetuity.

You can thus discern someone on what they produce for the future and you can know that when you don't produce in a way that's unselfish—that's for the nourishment of fellow humans—you get bottled up. You inflate with emptiness. The "living waters" that God sends back up once again.

Is your tree producing good fruit or cracking at the bark, with weak foliage? If it is the latter, it could be because you are not unleashing what God wants to send through you. You're holding something in. Something is bottling you up. It could be sin. You may be bloated—"puffed up"—with pride. You could be ready to explode due to a lack of lack of patience. You could be forcing things out of season.

Are you stretched to the limit? Are you "up to here"? Is your wood gnarled and ready to rot? The "waters" within you are clogged.

Only when the Holy Spirit flows freely through and from us can we expect miracles—and when we do, boy can we expect them! The fruit flourishes and returns; it multiplies! *Health comes to us as God moves from our roots through our branches to others.*

Let that flow.

The more you release, the more He sends. Release all anger. Release all hurts. Produce nothing you would not want to present to Jesus. Let His waters cleanse you.

This is true health. Here you will find balance.

Let go and let God and you will draw nutrients and bear fruit with Him forever.

32

Humility Drives Spirits Away and Builds a Shield Against Fiery Darts of Others

Another key: forsake worldliness.

Are you willing to downsize? Do you not see the benefit in a humbler, more meditative life? Can you learn to be less dependent on the world and more on His Providence?

Pray your way above the reality that we call earth. Pray yourself above emotionality. Pray your way above an instinctual negative reaction. Pray your way above the circumstances that irritate you and look down on them.

To resurrect is to leave things behind. It's to rise above the dynamics of this world and unite with Jesus Who will provide what you need. Be a rock. Let the rough water go around you. Don't be wood, which can float downstream. Certainly, we don't want to be cardboard (which the "water" goes right through), nor metal that rusts.

St. Peter was a "rock." Like Christ, he rose above hurt. Those caught up with His Spirit in the early Church transcended even torture.

Do the economists know what is occurring? They do not. Does government? It is wrapped in itself. Only God knows, and He will raise you above it (as well as provide).

Unite with Him. Keep Him in every thought. *Do everything for Jesus.* The answer is there.

Even in everyday life: when someone is rude or insulting or hurtful (these emotions are bound to increase), rise above them. Transcend in prayer. Let them not attach to old wounds. Do you realize how many things sting you because they're touching a weak point—touching a nerve that's still exposed?

Throughout life, we incur wounds as a result of broken relationships, harsh words, unfair conduct, deception, rejection, loss, and sin. There are wounds, and new problems can reopen them.

"The love and power of Christ healed people, and Jesus wants to heal us today," writes Father Dwight Longenecker, author of *Praying the Rosary for Inner Healing.* "His love can penetrate our lives and touch the wounds in our lives that are in areas so deep we don't even know about them. Do you remember the woman who crept up in the crowd to touch the hem of Jesus' cloak? She was forgiven and healed of a deep inner illness (see *Matthew* 9:20-22)."

When we have a confessed a sin but still enjoy the *memory* of it, we're attached to it, and here is bondage to the earth. Cleanse your spirit of lurid past behavior. Ask the Lord to wash away past evil thoughts. The purity of love is the air under your wings.

When we are attached to God through constant prayer, when we truly let our spirits move beyond emotions, when we "step outside" of ourselves (in humility, with unconditional caring), we transcend to levels of which we have not even dreamed and see that "dark" times are just clouds we pass through. Often in life, we're mystified by the way people react to us. There may be a sudden, inexplicable antagonism. Suddenly, it seems like the world is against us. There are antagonisms at home. There is tension at work.

Nobody seems to like us. In certain cases, a spirit that's in or around someone is reacting against us—or a spirit that has attached itself to *us* is causing antagonism.

Something unseen has latched onto us.

Many kinds of spiritual forces surround us and when we die we'll be astonished at what was at work at various points in our lives. There can be demonic or earthbound spirits "haunting" us, and the key is to cleanse.

On a daily basis, we should ask Christ and His Blessed Mother to sanitize the environment around us and purify our souls.

"Let God take any pain or trauma from your birth experience and heal it through the perfect birth of Jesus Christ at Bethlehem," says Father Longenecker. "Allow the pain and trauma of childbirth to be taken away. Let any distress or danger, fear or anxiety, be swept away in the loving confidence of St. Joseph and the totally unconditional love of Mary, your mother. Allow yourself to be 'born again' in this way, and have any gaps completed and fulfilled. Rest in the healing love of Christ, and allow the Holy Spirit to work His healing through your whole life over time."

The injuries are often the result of our own pride.

"How have you been humiliated?" asks Father Longenecker. "Have you been unappreciated, unrecognized, and cast to one side? Have family members, friends, and colleagues taken you for granted, mocked your ideas, or laughed at your hopes and dreams? Has someone attacked the very heart of your personality by finding what you most treasure and mocking it? Have you seen your dreams and hopes end in disappointment? Has your bitter disappointment been made worse by the seemingly successful lives of others? Do you feel their success burning in your own wound like a bitter fire?"

When that happens, we have pride to purge.

We have areas where we have to forgive.

We have to approach God for His cleansing in a way that is honest and allows us to reveal all of our warts, notes the priest.

That honesty chases spirits away.

Our "wounds" close.

They can't "hook" into us.

When folks react to you adversely, seek first to cleanse your interior being—then "break" and cast away what may be attaching into your weakness.

As you forgive (make a list), you'll actually feel burdens lift.

Your secret weapon: humility.

Humbleness drives spirits away from you—and builds a shield that quenches the darts that come from others.

When you are wronged, admonish with love. This will bear the greatest strength. Your correction will be more potent.

"As you meditate on the humiliation of Jesus as He is mocked and crowned with thorns, bring your own humiliations to Him," suggests Father Longenecker, referring to the healing Rosary. "In His Light, ask to see yourself clearly and honestly. Do you see how, in the midst of His humiliations, He looks on you with simple clarity, compassion, and love? He doesn't love you for your accomplishments or your gifts. He loves you simply for who you are."

The greater your problems, the greater potential there is for the future; the greater may be your destiny.

Who had greater destinies than Jesus, than Mary, and who had greater problems?

The key is to get *to* your destiny—and that means working through the challenge and being open to the Will of God (as was St. Anne, in whom the Immaculate Conception occurred, and then the Virgin herself, who then gave birth to

Jesus). It was the Lord telling God "Your Will be done, not Mine" that opened the way for the greatest destiny of all: our salvation.

When we confront and work through our problems (instead of complaining about them—or spending all our energy circumventing them) we too bear fruit. We too cleanse. Blessed was Mary's fruit! Blessed is our fruit when we allow the Holy Spirit to come through and pour forth from us. Our fruits define us.

That means using our gifts—to the maximum.

Your gifts produce your fruits and your fruits are who you really are; they are what is "in the wash"; they are the end product.

That comes only when we are constantly open to the Holy Spirit as was Mary. It means planting yourself in the right place, seeing the sun as much as possible, making sure you are firmly rooted, and cooperating with what is around you.

The more we yield, the more God sends, and the more He sends through us, the healthier we are (despite the challenges of physical or emotional pain, which are challenges).

The more we smile through pain, the more blessings He sends us.

33

Don't Let Stress Impede You

There are many gifts in life. Do you use yours to their fullest?

The more we use our muscles, the firmer they get. You'll be amazed at the pleasant turns in your life when you are yielding fruit at full throttle without second-guessing. (Constantly, there will be good surprise.) When we don't produce—when we're not using all our gifts, on all cylinders—there can be a block that causes failures, disappointments, or illness (the non-redemptive kind). We're "stopped up." There is lack of meaning. There's anxiety. We are stagnant. There is frustration.

Flush that away by using your gifts and producing like a valuable plant—not necessarily a plant that yields the best-looking fruit on the surface, but a plant that yields the largest healthful crop. God gives you all the gifts you need to work through problems and reach your destiny.

There are trials in life but joy comes more frequently to those who are doing all they can to bless others with the gifts God has given them.

What are your gifts? How do you use them? How *often* do you use them?

There is the gift of patience. There is the gift of prayer. There is the gift (above all) of love.

Ask the Holy Spirit what your gifts are and ask Him to guide you in how to use them. For when you use them to the fullest, you are not only bearing cleansing fruit that brings you closer to the immaculate but fulfilling something that is crucial: your life mission!

When you can't, when you remain blocked, you must ask yourself: Is it because you are trying to do something good (and the devil is resisting you), or because you are trying to do something that's not designed for you?

Ask yourself honestly.

Often, stress is a sign that we are overextended and it is the spirit telling us this through resistance.

Are you tense? When does it occur? How often? *How* does it occur? Around whom? In what circumstances? What might your inner spirit—your hidden self—be indicating?

As Father Longenecker asked, "Do you suffer from some weakness or failure that you can't seem to get the victory over? Do you fall into physical sin of which you are ashamed and embarrassed? You mean well, and you want to live in the full power and glory of Christ's Resurrection, but do you drift back into old habits, old negative ways of seeing yourself and others, old negative emotions and attitudes?"

If so, there could be hidden damage weighing on you—holding you in bondage.

Dr. Kenneth McAll who wrote books on ancestral healing focusing on concealed forces that can cause mental, emotion, and actual physical illnesses.

Life is a test at every turn, and there are startling ways that Satan can touch us.

Throughout this journey on earth—but especially in youth—exposure to risqué movies, video games, television programs, or pornography itself can cause lasting hidden damage. In our time, even cartoons have been tinged with the occult. *Such exposure can not only influence our desires and distort our conceptions* but also open us to damage by spirits that lurk for just that purpose.

The result can be loneliness, failure in relationships, and bad "luck" of all sorts.

Have you been damaged in ways you never really thought about by what your eyes have seen and ears have heard? What have you brushed up against?

Have books in your past—not only about sex, but also violence, the occult, or drugs—left a rent in your spirit?

When we're exposed to evil in music, we can be bound to that music. When we are exposed to the evil in a movie, we can be bound to the movie—or at least dinged in a way we don't see. When we do drugs, demons can enter. In the Bible it speaks not about occasional affliction but of "many" demons. Jesus cast them out everywhere He went.

There is a rule in God's Kingdom and it is that sinful behavior can lead to serious physical results. Take abortion. It has been linked, ironically, to breast cancer—the very capability to feed that infant which will not now come into existence.

That's a blatant example. Most are not. Satan often operates in what seems most innocent. Evil has touched almost everything. Everything seems upside-down. Evil has been made to seem good. You can't get away from the occult. Articles have recently focused on the history of the doll "Barbie"—which, it turns out, was fashioned in the 1950s after a popular adult German cartoon that featured a German prostitute doll name Bild Lilli and was considered by its creator as a sexual instrument.

Has that affected generations of women (and men)? Are seeds planted? How many movies and songs have oriented us in a direction that causes us spiritual issues—perhaps of the permanent kind? How many have been affected by *Playboy* or *Cosmopolitan*?

Go through all the songs of your youth and let the Holy Spirit inform you. Think again about some of the lyrics. Think of a movie and cast out any dark residue in the Name of Jesus.

Free and heal me, oh Lord. Think of songs. *Free and heal me, oh Lord.* Think of relationships. Free and heal . . .

If you abused drugs or alcohol or sex, seek deliverance from what happened through those portals. Go over every possible exposure—not with paranoia, but with the Rosary.

"Did you do anything that has never been confessed that you are ashamed of?" asked Father Longenecker. "Did you experiment with sin or indulge in destructive behaviors that you have never brought to Confession? All these things may still cloud your vision, impede your sense of vocation, and cause hurt, stress, illness, and a kind of spiritual handicap in your life."

Actual physical ailments.

The good news is that through Christ—and especially Communion (or the Rosary, as Father Longenecker points out)—we can go back through our lives, ask the Holy Spirit to roam over what we were exposed to, and let Him lead us to prayers of deliverance—title by title, lyric by lyric, movie by movie, the ones that were negative.

"Ask God to bring them to mind, and then take them to Confession to experience real healing and forgiveness," says Father Longenecker. "Imagine and experience the waters of your own baptism, as the grace of God washes through your life and cleanses the early adult years, and gives you a renewed sense of vocation and purpose in life."

Go through every single movie or photo or program you should not have watched, rebuke it, and cast it away until it has no sensual hold—until you feel release from it .

Then repair the injury.

The freedom you feel will surprise (and exhilarate) you.

The deliverance may change the course of your emotions!

Depression will usually leave.

Have you let the Lord shine His Light into the hidden parts of your spirit? It is very important. Have you gone in prayer through our memories and renounced what needs to be renounced—asking forgiveness, breaking that which binds us, and casting darkness away?

We build inner chambers throughout our lives and they reflect the places where we will stay in eternity.

Do you go to Confession monthly? Are you trying to keep your deepest parts clear (through repentance, forgiveness, and love)? Have you prayed to reveal the hidden areas where darkness may still lurk—causing mysterious blockages or even illnesses?

"For there is nothing hidden except to be made visible," said Jesus (*Mark* 4:21-25), "nothing is secret except to come to light."

Go through your soul and cleanse it as you do the rooms in your house. Clear the floors. Polish the tarnished brass. Create a sanctuary. Adore in those places and they will become as an Adoration chapel.

Pray with the saints. Pray with Mary. Ask the Lord to reveal the secret chambers of your soul, and then ask Jesus to purify them. With that the air will clear and you see into your destiny.

Work at selflessness, for it is a real power which brings that direct communication.

For when we are selfish, we have trouble seeing the spiritual forces—good or evil—that swirl around us.

Three ways of tapping into the good force are living for others, repenting, and learning to make sacrifices.

You'll note that those who have done that have a nearly indescribable quality about them. This is the magnetism and radiance that comes upon those who dedicate themselves to God, and a pattern of fortunate events hovers about them. Even animals seem attracted to them.

They suffer like everyone else (they too are tested) but they attract goodness. Do you recall those photos of doves swirling around Pope John Paul II and the miraculously dignified way that he died (his last word was "amen")?

There was no fear. We can get rid of fear if we are close to God through unselfishness. Perfect love casts out fear.

And it starts by stepping out of your "self." In other words, turn the ship around and have as your horizon a wider viewpoint. In everything you contemplate, begin your process of decision-making on how best to positively impact other people. See through their eyes. Hear with their ears. Imagine their sorrows, their trials. "Love your neighbor as yourself." Most importantly, consider everything you do in light of how it serves God.

Envision yourself stepping out of your self and view yourself as one of many all tied into a spiritual structure that serves the Lord. If there are blocks in your life, they may have a root in self-centeredness.

Don't take the "I" but the "we" perspective. Look at it as stepping out of sullied clothes. Throw yourself into a commitment to better others. Most of the time when we are unnerved it's because of something that concerns the ego.

Expurgate that and it will lead you to the second key, an attitude of sacrifice: Whatever you are about to do, view it as an offering. You have heard this before. Now act on it. Offer to God everything you do in life—from brushing your teeth to taking out the garbage. God especially likes to receive those things we dislike.

Be "born again."

That is, regain the purity and true manliness or womanliness with which you were born and like a baby, love and reach (and smile) without holding back.

34

Leaving Past Baggage

When we convert—when we actively go to Jesus—we leave transgressions.

The spiritual blinders lift.

We see "backstage" in the dynamics of life and there is no going back—or shouldn't be.

Too often, however, a part of us remains stuck in history. This brings us to another aspect of purging our histories: forgiving ourselves. Do you realize how frequently we hold ourselves back out of guilt? Do you spend time hovering over what you once did (before conversion)—past mistakes? Do you have trouble forgiving yourself (even after correcting the impulse that led to the misstep)?

If so, you need to rectify this. You need to clear your conscience. It's a dark cycle.

Like Lot fleeing Sodom, there is often the temptation for us to stop and review from whence we have come, a temptation to dwell on what we have fled (or see what is happening there). This is detrimental. Like Lot, there should be no looking back.

"As dawn was breaking, the angels urged Lot on, saying, 'On your way! Take with you your wife and your two daugh-

ters who are here, or you will be swept away in the punishment of Sodom.' When he hesitated, the men, by the Lord's
mercy, seized his hand and the hands of his wife and his two
daughters and led them to safety outside the city. As soon as
they had been brought outside, he was told: 'Flee for your
life! Don't look back or stop anywhere on the Plain'"
(Genesis 19).

To dwell on the past is to drive with mirrors. It's to see
things in reverse. When we look in a mirror things are not
quite as they seem. Past upsets? Hateful things? Are you still
on the "plain"?

Attach yourself to His Story, not history.

Otherwise, you become stuck. You risk turning into a
"pillar of salt." Or perhaps "ice" is the better way of saying
it, since you can become "frozen" in time. But once we've
done that, once we have brought each one to the Lord, we
can forget the mistakes themselves. We need not obsess on
them. The devil is the one who wants us to do this, and as
the saying goes, when the devil reminds you of your past,
remind him of his future.

Once the motive—the sin—is removed (through Confession, expiation, and resolution), it should be erased. *Leave
behind past transgressions and relationships* (especially
when the tie was sin). Take to the Eucharist anything that
still hangs you up and break each bond when the Host is
raised. Neither be curious about the world and the worldliness you left.

You are not who you were but who you are. When we
look at the negative side of our personal histories, what
happens? Think about it. We are tempted to relive past lusts,
past waywardness, past sins. We may even luxuriate in evil.

After you have prayed to heal whomever you may have
hurt, once you have purged, once you are reconciled, allow
God to brighten your horizon. If you have corrected a fault,

forget it and move on. Pray to have any hurt you caused remedied and then begin healing your own spirit.

Have the angels lead you (as they led Lot).

Jesus told us to take our ploughs and not look behind us and that's what the aim of conversion, which lasts a lifetime, must be: looking forward only to the future and Him.

Get over it—not under it. Don't let your past trap you. Live forward, not in reverse. Would you drive down an interstate backwards? Set your eyes on the highway to Heaven.

For when you are free of past guilt you are free to rise to Him.

Remember the old expression, *"Today's the first day of the rest of your life"?* It is. Never get stuck in your past.

Learn the "power of now." Live the best you can in the present.

Once you've acknowledged (and corrected) a past wrong, *let it go.* Stop punishing yourself. You're looking in the wrong direction.

Let's say you've had trouble relating with someone. You just can't seem to connect. You can't seem to get along. There may have been words that you regret, maybe just your attitude, which you wish could have been different, which you would like to relive.

Don't obsess on it; don't keep playing scenarios over and over. Love the person and move to the "now."

It does nothing to endlessly rehash what has occurred, and if you can project love toward a person who has troubled you, that's what God is looking for. He'll do the rest.

It's true that everything we've done and said and even thought in life counts and that one day we'll see our lives in review (like a movie); but this review won't focus on mistakes that we *corrected.*

Once that's been done, move on from the lesson.

It's the devil who tries to discourage. Let's get back to having a problem getting along with someone. There may be baggage. You may still be bound to the person. There may even be hatred. *There is a negative soul tie.*

You are free only if you've resolved in your heart to love and forget. It's not true that we can forgive without forgetting. Both are necessary. Don't replay what they said or you said or anyone said.

Move on. Erase it. Sweep away the residue, the memories. Remember that the Crucifixion was key but also that God moved to Resurrection from the Cross instead of remaining nailed to it. Look how the thief on Calgary was able to find Heaven by turning his life around in an instant of the "present." Remember, Jesus did not say "I was" or "I will be." He said, "I am."

Move forward with love and the power of God will overcome obstacles and purge that tension. When we fret over how others view us, we get stuck. Ask God to go back and straighten out what needs to be straightened, then move forward and don't worry about what anyone thinks of you. You can't make the water move back over the dam.

Don't replay mistakes. Let God go back in time and straighten it out. He is a time traveler. You are not. *Shut off negative internal dialogue.* Don't keep talking yourself down. Let God help you to halt thoughts from circulating in repetition like the neon ticker in Times Square (which goes nowhere).

Some say they forgive but can not forget and they fool themselves because they are still in bondage. When negative thoughts recur, stop the video tape. Put your heart, not your head, in the matter and edit it. Think with the best part of your spirit.

God knows you'll make mistakes. He doesn't expect you to be perfect. He *does* expect you to try to be perfect and when you're not to learn from what you did wrong and move forward.

If you can do that—if you can focus solely on present goodness, expanding it, wishing others the best—time whirls into a single force of love that heads toward God.

When we right a wrong—with our whole hearts—in God's Eyes (after expiation) it is changed. Did you waste time? Did you neglect things? Have you offended (who has not)? Go back and ask God to fix that too. Pray that the results He expected occur despite your lapse.

You'll feel harmony. Relief. Why harbor anxiety?

Ask Mary and the Lord to unknot your past. Make things right. Turn radiant.

35

Don't Let the Devil Push You Off Balance

You'll have that brightness when you have *balance*.

Maria Esperanza often taught that a crucial component in life is balance. It is the key to so many things! It's a key to peace. It is a key to joy. It is a key to health. In the end, it is the key to happiness.

Take a look at what "balance" means.

It means not to go to any one extreme. It means to make sure you tend equally to all aspects of your life. It means not going too far in anything.

Are you too complacent, too anxious? Are you lazy or a workaholic? Do you talk too little—or too much? Do you love or are you over-attached?

Are you balanced in the way you parcel out your time? Do you spend as much time with your loved ones as on the computer or at work or in front of the television? Do you balance labor with rest, love with correction, physical attraction with spiritual love?

Often to balance means to find a middle ground or the crux of the fulcrum.

There is a balance between wealth and poverty, nourishment and gluttony, inactivity and burning oneself out.

Too much (or too little) of anything tends toward darkness.

The devil is a man of extremes.

Note the scales of justice. Note the balanced way of saints.

Note, too, the teeter-totter: when one end is too heavy or too light, it doesn't go anywhere. On one seat a person is stuck to the ground while at the other a person is left up in the air. It comes down with a bang.

With balance (which comes with discipline and prayer), we can do anything. We can accomplish the impossible. We can cross a chasm. Take a tight-rope walker: Isn't it amazing how a person can walk on a thin rope over a gorge or between skyscrapers by practicing perfect equilibrium?

Talk about the straight and narrow! When we have balance, we're eating the right things. We're following a balanced approach. This is why nutrition is so confused: researchers constantly seek to discover magical formulas to health when all they need is to ask God for the gift of balance. He will tell you what is good for you and in what proportion. It is different for everyone.

When we have balance, we have the full fruits of the Spirit and even the results of your kitchen efforts possess an extra "something." Besides her fantastic gifts and very busy life (tending to endless visitors), Maria found enough time to cook extraordinary meals, bake unusually tasty desserts, and make every single member of her family feel so special that they never wanted to leave her side (sometimes more than thirty would travel with her to the States).

When the Holy Spirit is present, we do everything well and anything delightful can happen. For balance, look to Jesus. He drank but he was no lush. He ate, but also, He fasted. He admonished but loved. Everything multiplied around Him!

Often, we are attacked by darkness because we lack equilibrium. We're too narrow. We're too intent on one thing or another. We tip the ship because we're obsessed.

When we have balance, we're not extremists. We're not closed-minded. We are religious but open. We are even-handed. We think before we talk. We are not Pollyannas but neither are we negative.

Prayer. Humility. They can change your life. For when you have balance, the Holy Spirit surrounds you not only with well-being (an exquisite feeling) but also with His protection.

Don't let the devil push you off balance.

Don't let him take away your focus.

36

Don't Let the Devil Misdirect

Call this a "law of the crows": The devil often tries to divert our focus for a crucial moment and often does so as we approach a threshold or intersection.

A threshold of holiness. A threshold of advancement.

I recall driving and being distracted one time by a crow that bounded on the street, and then another that bounced in a strange manner—in a similar attention-getting fashion—just across the way, as if to steal our attention.

The temptation, of course, was to switch the eyes to them and off the road and paying too much notice to those birds could have caused an accident. We were also approaching a crossroads. There was two-way traffic.

Often Satan works to trip us up not by way of a frontal attack (which is what we usually expect) but in the way of a side show. It can be a squirrel. It can be another car. In life, it's usually something that's none of our business.

He comes at the periphery. He is barely in view. He seeks to sway your glance long enough to cause you to go in a wrong direction.

We see this when it divides us, when it slanders, when it leads to sin, when we regress spiritually. Those are times we can discern the devil's effects. He is the great deceiver, and a ploy of a deceiver is misdirection (ask any magician). Evil is where evil lies and so we watch at the periphery of the road for what is peculiar, what's artificial, what is too spectacular, which is where you will find falsehood. It is diversionary. It has a sales pitch. The devil is a liar and he *lies* in wait (like the snake that he is).

Don't always expect him to come in an obvious manner. Watch for his suddenness.

How many times has the devil diverted you? How many times has he made you pay attention to something trivial when there were more important matters? How much time has he caused you to waste? How many times in your life have you missed opportunities or failed to note a problem because you were paying attention to something else—were distracted? The cock crows thrice and so does the crow.

We all have intersections in life—more than we realize—and we approach them in the right fashion only when we have clear vision and are looking (through prayer) straight ahead; when we don't take our eyes off the ball (or the road).

Now, there are times that God blocks us. There are times we are headed the wrong way and He tries to nudge us in the right direction. This we must discern.

But it can also be Satan. He sends people to block us, to put up a stop sign, to place a red light where we are not meant to stop or turn. The attacks often come from those who are familiar and thus in ways we least expect. (Look at how through Peter the devil tried to divert Jesus.)

Too often, we let others make the decisions for us. This also is a problem at intersections!

This too—indecision—the devil sends. Look straight ahead and always turn back to your direct path when something crops up on the side of you. Let Jesus be your guide, always. When it happened to Him, He said, "Get thee hence!"

37

You are a Person of Destiny

Approach every day with the Rosary and the devil will lose this device. In prayer you will spot the diversions. Look for the Light in prayer (first thing in the morning) and remember that His Light does not divert because light does not bend.

While we easily see evil in the way of crime and abortion, we rarely take note of how it manifests in the way of disorientation. The great manifestation of our culture is precisely this. We see it at all levels. Disorientation is when, for example, those in our society who are very compassionate in other ways support a "right"—abortion—that is a genocide.

This is true disorientation: when the well-intentioned or seemingly well-intentioned are deceived and tend to evil without knowing it. It has afflicted us all. It affects the liberal as well as the conservative. It is obvious in those too who fight abortion but promote war. Recently, the disorientation has been noted in *L'Osservatore Romano* when a columnist for this Vatican newspaper gave a glowing review to the latest Harry Potter movie, even though there is all but ironclad proof that the Harry Potter books have caused an explosion in teen witchcraft.

When good is evil and evil is good, this is the disorientation of our times and we all go through periods of blindness—whereby we can see all that is wrong with others without noting the blots in our own spirits. When a devout person exhibits hostility and lacks charity (often over a religious matter), this too is disorientation.

The answer is prayer and purging those blots: self-deliverance, through pleas to the Holy Spirit.

In prayer, we can see the truth.

In prayer, I can't overemphasize, we can see more clearly.

You can never be too busy to pray.

If in your life you feel confused, pray to see the entire truth of your circumstance. Pray to see yourself from all sides. Pray to see yourself as God sees you.

One day, we will all see our lives in review, and we can pray now to know how to make that review a pleasant one.

When we are disoriented, we fear getting lost. This is the root of anxiety.

You are a person of destiny. You are destined for Heaven. You are destined to be the best you can be. That is your direction.

You are also unique. Period. Your greatness is not worldly greatness.

And so your soul bears God's secret imprint.

You could also call it a road map. Let's talk about destiny, which also means destination. Everyone has one. We are not talking about being a great Hollywood star or a famous athlete. We are talking about accomplishing God's Plan in the ordinary walk of life. To God, this is true greatness!

That plan was written before you were born. It's etched into your deepest subconscious. Somewhere, deep down, you know what you are supposed to do; you know where you are supposed to go; you know the plan for your life. It would defeat the "test" of life to know it consciously.

And so it is hidden but for brief moments at deep levels when our souls gain contact with God.

The Lord has a *right destiny* in mind for each of us and the trick, again, is to reach it with the purity and love of a child. When we do that, our task has been completed.

If we can do that, we can gain direct heavenly entry.

Life is the road. There are turns. There are curves. There are ravines. There are confusing road signs. There is *dirt*. There are deserts. Also, there are mountains. We can make it over a mountain or fall off the summit (or never reach it).

There are creatures at roadside.

The key is to pray from the heart each day for God's Will *with indifference to material things.* This is what St. Ignatius of Loyola taught us. Wish not for wealth or poverty.

Why so many twists and turns in life? As one writer noted, God created opposing pairs such as black and white, long and short, healthy and sick, so we can experience everything. Fire can cook our dinner or burn us. Water can quench your thirst, give life to plants, or destroy fields.

It is not that fire and water are evil but how we approach them.

And so too the "curves" in the road of life, the script and design of our secret imprint. If we make it past the twists and turns we transcend sorrow (and avoid regret).

When we operate in accordance with God's "imprint," we have wisdom beyond our years; we accomplish more than we thought we would; things fall into place. When we exercise *excellence and integrity* in fulfilling the plan He has for us, we are suddenly "at the right place at the right time."

It's not by coincidence that good things happen but because God has seen that you are keeping to His course and has intervened.

The natural is taken over by the supernatural. Think big and God will act big—in the right way.

As the preacher put it, God doesn't match you to the size you think you are, but the size of your destiny—and gives what you need to accomplish every dream He put into your heart. When you are fully in the walk of destiny, your voice will have the tone of an angel. *If God is with you, who can be against you?*

You are equipped and well able to overcome anything that is placed on the road. The trouble is when *we* go off onto side routes, when we try to map out every detail of our lives, when we seek shortcuts (usually to avoid pain), when we seek worldly greatness (instead of the greatness He has imprinted).

Then everything is uphill; the possible becomes impossible! We constantly fall into ravines (and blame God).

Just remember to seek His imprint and know that the size of problem is not as important as the size of the person. If the greatest power of the universe is in you, where is there room for fear?

Always remember that no matter what has (or has not) happened in your life, *you still have every seed of greatness that you were born with.*

You can regain the path.

You can (still) make your destination.

When you spend the potential God has equipped you with—when you release all gifts, when you fulfill your God-given destiny, when you seek to do His Will and His alone—all potential is refreshed.

The goal in life is to align our plans for life with what God planned long ago (and stick to it). Do your best day in and day out. You'll be surprised at wisdom beyond your years and how you accomplish more than you even wanted to! Think big and He will act big. Look for the ultimate destiny. Do the right thing even when the "wrong" thing is happening.

You know how hard it can be to pull the cord on a lawn mower? But that's what life necessitates: a constant startup each day as we traverse the course God has set before us. (Sometimes it starts with a lot of noise!)

Just pull the cord; never mind the "negatives."

It is all He asks. Perhaps He plans certain successes for you. Perhaps certain trials. Just stick to it. Persist. Regain hope. Maintain the right dream. Live by *His* blueprint.

Be like Jesus; seek to complete your task. Reach the point He did, whereby He could look toward Heaven and at the end of His course say, "It is finished."

Seek the "robe of Heaven." What's the robe of Heaven? That means: the *deepest* you. Do you know the deepest part of yourself? Or have you allowed life to silt it over? It's the one God created you to be—the "best version of yourself." It's the "you" He will recognize.

When it's obscured, it could mean purgatory. We really do "wear" what is deepest within us into Heaven! Listen to what a woman named Angie Fenimore who died and saw deepest purgatory alleged. "Drifting onto the plane, the newly deceased were dressed in white robes, but their robes were dingy," she wrote (in *Beyond the Darkness*). "Like silent sleepwalkers, these spellbound souls descended into the darkness, arms to their sides, their expressionless eyes locked in empty gazes. Everyone I saw was wearing dirty white robes. Some people's were heavily soiled, while others' just appeared dingy with a few stains."

Or listen to this from a revelation called *The Secrets of Purgatory*:

"The souls in purgatory are enveloped, as it were, in a thick shroud into which they have wound themselves while living on this earth," says the incredible little booklet. "It is the garment of their own egoism. Their main care in this life was themselves, just as the world's highest ideal is self-glorification and honor. It is this which fashions that coarse garment through which the Light of God can hardly penetrate."

In eternity, there are no secrets. We wear who we (really) are.

There was the you as a youngster: encountering your first temptations. How did you do? Are there still things you must purge? Do those memories haunt or entice? There was the you as a teenager—more temptations, many more, still. And in that critical period of your twenties. What stains did you pick up? There is the "you" who became a spouse, a parent, a grandparent, the you who chose a certain career.

What were your intentions? How many masks have you worn? Did anything "crust" around you? Do you still harbor—wear—any bitterness? Is there hardness?

The real you is the you at your most comfortable, your most natural, your purest, your happiest.

What sullies us?

The best you is not the complainer. It's not the one who sees the worst in others. It's not the *lackadaisical* you. It's not the one who lives by force. Stains indeed! It's not a gossip.

Let's focus on that for a moment.

"In over two decades of ministry, I've encountered scores of Christians who don't seem to think gossip is wrong—who are obsessed as busybodies, gossips, and bad-mouthers, and have caused irreparable damage to the Body of Christ," wrote one evangelist.

"I could fill books with the stories of anguish and grief inflicted to hapless victims. 'The words of a gossip are like choice morsels; they go down to a man's inmost parts' (*Proverbs* 26:22). Mean, vicious accusations and rumors have ripped out the heart and soul of many fellow Christians and leaders, draining them of their love, enthusiasm, and their desire to live for God. It has split churches, created strife, and promoted division and turmoil. 'Without wood a fire goes out; without gossip a quarrel dies down' (*Proverbs* 26:22).

"Gossip exists whenever persons 'talk about others' in less than a favorable way. The root of gossip is negativity, judgmentalism, slander, etcetera. Avoid associating with people who gossip. 'A gossip betrays a confidence; so avoid a man who talks too much' (*Proverbs* 20:19). You probably remember the old saying: 'If you can't say something good about others, don't say anything at all.' Wise advice if you wish to avoid sin.

"Gossip often masquerades as 'concern' for others. Rumors or gossip will seem more palatable if they first hide behind a pretentious expression of concern. 'I hate to say anything about this to you, but I'm "concerned" about so and so.' At other times the gossiper will seek you out as their 'confidante' to unload their 'heavy heart' about their concerns. 'I'm very troubled about so and so and I don't know who else to talk to about it.' In reality, the gossip is not sincerely concerned about solving the problem, only in talking about it—stirring it up. 'A perverse man stirs up dissension, and a gossip separates close friends' (*Proverbs* 16:28). A gossip thrives on the negative, the controversial, and the sensational. Any person who is genuinely concerned about solving a problem will go and privately confront the person at the source and express their concern. Or else they should go privately to the pastor so he will do it."

Wow.

Inner turmoil is reflected by the hidden corners in our homes, where dirt collects. What is within us is without us. The dust builds up if we don't constantly take care of it.

The more we pray, the more discipline we have—and this is the key to upkeep and the "best version of you," is it not?

When there is a lack of prayer, dust gathers.

Prayer is discipline and translates into the discipline we have over the flesh and even over our personal upkeep.

If, as some say, negative spirits seem to gather around clutter and confusion, a sign of their presence may thus be in what is scattered—or piled—around us. *What's around us reflects our passions and shortcomings and also our obsessions.* Those who have become obsessed with objects become—at an extreme—the hoarders we see on television. Meanwhile a person obsessed with drugs or alcohol can become the homeless street person who has no energy or discipline for upkeep. (Is this why there is the saying that "cleanliness is next to Godliness"?)

On the upside: our surroundings can reflect goodness and togetherness and joy. That's your best version of you for sure!

The truth of love is happiness.

Love transcends all sorrow.

It also transcends criticality.

The best version of us sees the best in others.

Gauge the *real you* by that standard.

Do you want to appear before God all dented up, dusty, as a rusted old jalopy—or waxed and ready to shine?

We have to simply start *doing*. When we are doing nothing we are going nowhere. Inertia takes over.

When we neglect our cars, we risk breakdown. When we obscure our real selves, the Lord may say He doesn't know us (*Luke* 13).

Do. Start a motion. *Move.*

Build momentum.

Make that first start.

Lust? That's a stain. Half-truths? Blotches on your robe. Constant complaining? Negativity? Discontent? A dark hue. Hatred? Blackness.

Be careful what you let into your eyes and ears? It will express itself outwardly.

As the most popular televangelist, Joel Osteen, says, "Have you ever heard the saying, 'You are what you eat'? The same principle is true in our spiritual lives. Our ears and eyes are the gates to our soul. What we watch, what we listen to, and who we associate with are constantly feeding and influencing our inner man, which in turn, influences our actions and destiny. *Psalm* 119:37 says, 'Keep me from paying attention to worthless things.' David said in *Psalm* 101:3, 'I will set before me no vile thing.' Today more than ever, we have opportunities to feed our minds with the wrong thing. Everywhere we turn, there is information trying to influence us. But *Ephesians* 4:27 says, 'Do not give the enemy a foothold.'

"A door of opportunity is opened when we allow negative influences in our lives. What seems as harmless entertainment, a compromising TV show, or a negative song choice eventually influences your thought life. Thoughts lead to actions and actions determine your destiny. Spend time building yourself up, not wasting your time with activities that can tear you down. You are a temple of the Most High God—called, appointed, and anointed to do great things. Do your best to keep your temple pure and be selective with what you feed your spirit. As you do your part, God will take you places that you have never imagined. You will reach your full potential and become everything God has created you to be."

Cleanse, cleanse, cleanse.

Our example is Immaculate Mary.

Purity (sought with prayer from the heart) is the best *you* and will lead to a brilliant white robe that will radiate the love of God like a texture of spun cotton and spun glass.

38

Find and Be the Best Version of Yourself

There are seasons of struggle, and seasons of concern. There are seasons of favor. They all open to a new dimension of life when we go inwardly and "clean house"—when—before fixing the entire world—we search through the "rooms" in our own souls and check for dirt, for cobwebs, for jealousies, for resentment, for unforgiveness, hatred, pride, for lust, bias, for clumps of dust that prevent us from realizing the joy of the Spirit.

Open the doors to your soul with Christ and clean those inner chambers. Cleanse the vessel. Look at those rooms as vaults and place the Blessed Sacrament in each one. This will drive out sin which fuels trepidation.

Only when your interior vessel is clean can you partake fully of the Blood of Jesus.

Under the dirt in those rooms you will find hidden treasure.

Concern, yes; there are reasons to be *concerned*. There have been for years. We approach major events.

But fear? Anger?

They're related: Anger is mostly rooted in fear as many today have economic or societal or political worries and they threaten to cause something we have also repeatedly warned about: *a time of division* (and upheaval).

It doesn't have to occur. If it does, we can find peace, joy, and fearlessness with the Holy Spirit. Perfect love casts out all fear *even in chaos.* Stop being mad at everyone. The way of hatred is never the way of truth.

It has become a trend.

It's fashionable to attack everyone who has a different opinion.

It is also the route to evil.

Escape to the depth of prayer and shut off that which sacrifices goodness for the sake of debate. Don't fool yourself into *wrong righteousness.*

It's not introversion. It's not "copping out." It is not escapism.

It's calming down, casting away passions. It's turning off "the world" and letting the Holy Spirit speak to you as opposed to the rancor of media.

It's praying long enough for the Spirit to lead you into a state of inner rest and here you sense your mission. Here you find your secrets. It is where you can say, "God will get us through this" and "this shall pass," and it is where there is a font of *holy determination.*

A key to life is holy determination. Fill yourselves with that!

Determine not to fear but to use your eyes of faith to see a new season.

Discipline comes by embracing the Cross and brings the harmony of our faculties in proper proportion, which leads to true joy and a connection with God Who is bigger than any suffering and even bigger than joy. (Meditate on that!)

To carry the Cross is to let go of anxiety, of what the world is trying to foist upon you—*anger, self-righteousness, criticism.*

We are in difficult times. They will become more difficult. This we have known for many years. It's a challenging time, which also means it is an exciting time: affording all the more opportunity to cleanse. Autumn leads to winter which leads (recall always) to spring.

Tap not into your failings but the strength of your spirit. Jesus said, "Woe to you, scribes and Pharisees, you hypocrites. You are like whitewashed tombs, which appear beautiful on the outside, but inside are full of dead men's bones and every kind of filth. Even so, on the outside you appear righteous, but inside you are filled with hypocrisy and evildoing" (*Matthew* 23).

In other words: go inward, before going outward. Turn off the noise of the world.

Evil plays on both sides of the fence.

When we think we are right and everyone else is wrong it gives us the excuse *not* to self-correct, *not* to love, *not* to cleanse (when in fact that is desperately needed). This we see as the prelude to the current force of upheaval.

Have you prayed to rid yourself of generational baggage? Have you cleansed of the "bones" from past sins, from spirits that may hover within or about you: have you cast them from your inner chambers?

As a deliverance expert once said, the effect of straying from Him is seen when theology is exalted above revelation, intellectual education above character, psychology above discernment, eloquence above supernatural power, laws above love, and reasoning above the walk of faith.

"Whoever teaches something different and does not agree with the sound words of our Lord Jesus Christ and the religious teaching is conceited, understanding nothing, and has a morbid disposition for arguments and verbal disputes," says *1 Timothy* 6:2. "From these come envy, rivalry, insults, evil suspicions, and mutual friction among people with corrupted minds, who are deprived of the truth, supposing religion to be a means of gain."

When bad fruit comes from a person, it is often in the form of division, tension, anxiety, confusion, and hardness. Our spirits resist or even bristle at the proud. Pride is pretense and pretense is the first thing an exorcist must remove (before getting to the demonic). Pride yields the worst fruit because it grows in darkness. We can be deceived by fruit as we saw Eve and Adam deceived in the Garden.

When good fruit comes, it is in the way of peace, joy, and comfort. You feel at home with yourself. It is the effect the fruit has that figures into our tally.

What about our children? Are they "fruits"?

They have their own free will and so we can't be held accountable for everything they do. On the other hand, we are able to judge the Blessed Mother by the "Fruit" of her womb.

The best fruits come from our "highest self" (just like choice fruit is often up there on the top branches). What's meant by "highest self"?

It is the heart and mind joined in purity of intention. It's the "you" in wonderful moments when spiritual power seems at a peak around you. It is that time you seemed to have perfect inner sanctity—rising above the quibbles and aggravations of life, not letting anything or anyone bother you. It is that high point you have felt after the most powerful Communion. You transcend. You rise above.

Nothing disturbs you. You see everything in the proper context of eternity. Holy, holy, holy. This should be your goal. The difficulty: keeping at this level. You know how it is: you feel an ecstatic moment—you have a little epiphany, are feeling so well after Mass, everything seems to be going just right—and then someone comes along with a word or a look or an action (or an e-mail) or thoughtlessness and vacuums the anointing from you. Anything that takes a blessing from you is a fruit from darkness (where grows fungus).

Most of the time, this happens because we let our guard down, react to a negative, and adopt a wrong thought pattern (or "lower self"), letting emotions bubble to the surface of your soul.

If someone is producing bad fruit, remember that not everyone spiritually matures at the same time. We all have our "moment of understanding." A person who has hurt you may not yet have reached his moment. Always see the other person's side.

Purity toward one another is in the love we send. What fruit are we yielding? Are we bringing peace to others, are we bringing joy, or are we robbing happiness from others?

Are we creating peace or anxiety?

When we maintain our highest selves, we yield an abundance that gives health to our souls and to the souls of others which transmits into healing—even physically. At the high point, we transcend the world's trivialities (no matter how "important" they seem).

Let it go. The wind will blow. It will go away. Release, release, release. And say: Let no one be held in purgatory on my account.

Don't let grace be stolen. Don't eat the wrong fruit. Don't let people destroy your joy. Maintain the high point of your existence. At the same time, avoid a tree that is constantly yielding bitter fruit; it robs the good taste. View matters from the highest branch, which means constant selflessness despite trials that strengthen our roots and branches and leaves.

Humility is the "land of the brave." It is also the "lent" of the brave. It takes sacrifice but ends up with power. It takes a view that is spiritual instead of natural.

Big point here: spirit over nature.

Let's think here a moment over how the Lord prepared in the desert. He must have thought ahead to forgiveness from the Cross. It is so important to forgive. When we don't forgive someone, we are tied to the person—and to what the person has done. We have woundedness. We hide in our own wounds—instead of His.

Forgive. During Holy Week, but really every week, start a new "you." Begin a new way of life. Crucify the old self.

Also, forgive yourself. Did you know that those who have "deathbed visions" often accent the importance of forgiving oneself?

Without it, we are bound to the sin and may be bound to this earth.

Remember that Satan is the great accuser.

He wants to negate the power of the Cross.

On Good Friday—but really always—think back on everything for which you feel guilt and release it to God. Take all your sins and one by one place them in the wounds of Jesus. Forgive, forgive, and then forgive some more— opening the door to love of God, love of yourself (in the holy way), and love of others.

If you have trouble loving others, or in gaining peace (or healing), see if you need to shed guilt.

You can't love well if you can't love yourself (again, in an unselfish way).

Forgive yourself (after Confession) and move on.

I often mention the "living waters" and water is symbol- ized in the blue rays emanating from the image of Divine Mercy. So is Crucifixion. It's in the red rays and we can say that to receive the full grace or "waters" from the Lord, we too need crucifixion; we need to "crucify" the old self, the selfish nature, the old greedy self. We need—in other words—to take on a new nature.

Distance yourself from those who are from your unholy side, who feed the wrong self, and move on with your life. Also, distance yourself from that which afflicts you. Look at what surrounds you. "The things we love tell us who we are." Cleanse deeply.

Find out who you really are.

Often, we can't forgive ourselves because we don't remember our authentic selves and the reason we don't know who we really are is because we are always trying to be someone else.

Find peace in your role. Love what God wanted for you. Be the true you.

That's the best "you."

39

Take a Step Back from What Annoys You

What have been your intentions in life? How many masks have you worn? Did anything "crust" around you? Do you still harbor—wear—any bitterness?

Is there hardness (a shell)?

When we are in a shell, blessings bounce off of us. So does love. The real you is the you at your most comfortable, your most natural, your purest, your softest, your happiest; the real you gives and thrives on love.

A curse will not alight if the spirit is right.

"Like a sparrow in its flitting, like a swallow in its flying, so a curse without cause does not [land]," promises *Proverbs* 26:2.

A curse "hisses" at us. There is oppression. There is obsession. There is depression. *Stress.* At the extreme, there may be possession.

Father John Hampsch, who is expert in this field, adds *repression suppression, regression*, and *aggression*.

We *repress* when we hold back expressions of love. This gives the devil a toehold. We *regress* when we backslide—

lapsing into old ways (and less mature patterns). We *suppress* when we allow old hurts to remain. "This is like bandaging over a festering sore, without removing the infecting splinter," says the priest.

Are we oppressed by our thoughts?

Do we go in to funks from which we can't surface easily (depression)?

You cannot be cursed—even by a witch—if your soul is pure in its intentions.

Open the windows of your soul. Breathe in the Holy Spirit. Practice random acts of kindness. Take a step back from what annoys you. Look at it like a disinterested third party. Don't let irritations engage you.

If there is no darkness—no dirt, no wrong emotion—evil finds no place to hide; and hide in darkness it must.

A boy who had many experiences with angels as he was dying related Heaven to his doctor in an interesting way. Is Heaven like earth, he was asked by the doctor? "Yes," said the boy, "but it's perfect. It's like earth, but we finally get to live our lives without worry and have everything we want." He said the angels had granted him glimpses of paradise and that it is like "every day is your birthday."

We begin to live Heaven on earth, they tell us, when we aim for joy. Then, entering the afterlife is like walking into another room. "Remember, pray without ceasing," a woman who also experienced death says she was told (again, we presume, by angels). "Play, love, laugh, live for the joy of it. Have fun. Happiness is holy."

And, holiness makes us happy.

Joy is a sign that we are on the right path. Live it now. Taste Heaven, while on earth! Christ is "joy to the world."

Yes, we suffer in life. All of us. But it says in Scripture that sorrow is turned into joy (*John* 16:20) and when we love God with all our hearts there is joy even in pain; we note the huge smile on saints like Padre Pio (who "suffered" the stig-mata), or the way John Paul II glowed (even to the "bitter" end).

In fact, with Jesus, there *is* no bitterness. There is no fear. Fear comes when we are not entirely prepared for eter-nity (it is our soul letting us know).

To have joy is to get rid of jealousy, to stop competing so hard, to halt the race to get more than the next person, which robs both joy and peace. Instead, cooperate. Wish everyone the best. Find joy in their blessings!

Do you still feel in competition? Do you begrudge others?

If so, you may have to remove pride from your soul.

Remember what it says in Scripture: "God resists the proud."

Now follow it up with a responsorial psalm:

"Blessed the man who follows not the counsel of the wicked nor walks in the way of sinners, nor sits in the company of the insolent."

40

Ignore Those Who Try to Provoke You

When someone is trying to attack you, or trap you into a fight, or sting you with words, often the only solution is to ignore the person. And to do that, you must completely prevent yourself from delving into what the person is trying to drill into you.

If you are receiving darkness from someone, stop paying mind to it. Curiosity is the enemy. When you listen to or read something you know is unfair, that simply tempts you to act imprudently—and then to do what you were falsely accused of. When we tap into darkness, it can gush like a Gulf well.

On occasion, the Lord speaks loudly to all of us and often it is in warning. This we *don't* ignore.

The Lord may tell you to ignore a certain person who is known to cause disturbances. Shortly after, the person may do just that—and you succeed in obedience if you avoid the temptation of seeing what had been said. That brings grace because when we listen to a "word" from God, He sends more words. It strengthens the communication. It opens us to a new level of warning. Your fruit will match your growth.

When we don't heed what He tells us, He stops or slows down such communication.

To ignore is not to show disdain. It *is* to "disregard," and sometimes we have to disregard people—or at least what they try to tell us. It is the evil one behind it. It is meant to disrupt or engage us.

To ignore is to set aside or reject a "groundless indictment."

A groundless indictment is a false charge. It is taken from thin air. It is in the mind (or spirit behind) a person.

Look at it for what it is and don't let the devil speak to you. (The more you do, the more he will also!) Transcend it. Pray for the person. This puts a stop to it. Don't even skim read it. Don't look for a summary. Don't care to know, unless you truly did something wrong.

In life, we all go through groundless charges. We usually sense them in the spirit, and should go with that. Sometimes we are misunderstood. Sometimes, a person is simply nasty. Ignored, their stings recede. It is when we react in kind that it turns into a prolonged suffering.

Next time you see what seems like a poison pen note in the mail, or on Facebook, or in an e-mail, or a person tries to speak it to you, shut it off immediately, and totally; exercise discipline. Stop your curiosity from wanting to indulge in it. Once more, don't drink of the poison.

Instead, bide by the soft Voice of the Lord and He will whisper the gentleness that will sustain your spirit.

If something is plaguing you, ask the Holy Spirit to guide you in shutting off any source it may be coming from (without letting your imagination run wild). You may have a weak point allowing entry. Did you know that when negativity has collected around a person, that evil can be transmitted?

The most powerful way evil accumulates is through atheism, hatred, or vanity.

Let's focus on the last—which is a category of pride.

Few things are more potent than vanity, and few things are such a waste of time.

The word "vanity" comes from the Hebrew word for "vapor."

This is key. It tells us that like vapor, arrogance—self-conceit—does not last.

To be puffed up is to be full of nothing.

Vanity leads to jealousy and jealousy is one of the most common and powerful ways that spirits are telegraphed. As I have said, jealousy is a curse, and a curse is marshalling darkness to affect another.

To have vanity is to be vain and to be vain is to have ego which means pride which means a focus on one's own "stature." It is to focus on the self. It is to orient one's life to serve an appearance. Remember that painting of a skull in a vanity mirror?

It is to serve worldliness.

Worldliness is tabulating stature on the basis of physical objects and societal standing. As even the Blessed Mother has said, *"What does God desire of you? Do not permit Satan to open the paths of earthly happiness, the paths without my Son. My children, they are false and last a short while."*

The devil once appeared to this seer as an incredibly handsome man who offered the visionary "success in life and love" if she would follow him. She would only suffer, he lied, if she followed the Blessed Mother.

In another case, a man who "glimpsed" hell during a near-death experience said he saw a large red eye that showed him earthly temptations and an end to pain and anguish—if, like the seer, he would follow him. "Visions of wealth appeared before my eyes, like a three-dimensional movie," said this fellow. "Diamonds, money, cars, gold, beautiful women, everything."

The devil can anoint us—"bless" us with glamour, money, and worldly possessions. Did he not offer the kingdoms of the world to Jesus?

Many are those who consider rich or famous or powerful people to be blessed—but by which force?

And how have they used their riches?

To be worldly is to chase the wind because no matter what we collect in life, it vanishes like vapor at the end of life. Here we get back again to "vanity"! It is one of the great evils of our time—this era of reality shows and fifteen minutes of fame and an obsession with looks (to the point of surgically altering how God made us). "I have seen all the works which have been done under the sun, and behold, all is vanity and striving after wind," says *Ecclesiastes* 1:14.

"Men of low degree are only vanity and men of rank are a lie; in the balances they go up; they are together lighter than breath," adds *Psalm* 62:9.

Let's go back to the origin of these words.

Vanity, say etymology books, is "emptiness, foolish pride." It is "banal or excessive sentimentalism." It is "air in motion"—often, hot air. There is even "vain sorrow."

The prince of the power of the air is Satan and he collects around those who have pride. Believe this! They channel dark forces like conduits—*we* channel dark forces, when we let pride control our thoughts.

It is from vanity that jealousy comes and jealousy—says *Proverbs*—is even more powerful than anger. When a person has collected dark forces around himself and is jealous, those forces can be "transmitted" to the target of the jealousy and here we have a severe demonic attack ("who can stand in the face of jealousy," says *Proverbs* 27:4).

Vanity and jealousy go hand in hand and argue against love; they are the opposite; no one with a big ego is a big lover; no one with much vanity has a huge heart. It is only delusion to think so—and in this time of vanity, in the Age of Ego, it is important that we root out every manifestation of it.

Even in religion, those who feature themselves as holy develop a vanity that turns into a judgmental mindset that then devolves into criticality and a mean spirit that makes a mockery of Christ.

Vanity of vanities, says *Ecclesiastes*. "All is vanity"—all that makes for evil here and causes the soul to head for darkness after.

During an apparition, Mary once said, *"Free yourself of everything from the past which burdens you and gives you a sense of guilt; of everything that brought you to error—darkness. Accept the light. Be born anew in the justice of my Son."*

"I will help you to triumph over errors and temptations with my grace. I will teach you love, love which wipes away all sins and makes you perfect, love which gives you the peace of my Son now and forever. Peace with you and in you, because I am the Queen of Peace."

"Do not be afraid, my children, I am here with you, I am next to you. I am showing you the way to forgive yourselves, to forgive others, and, with sincere repentance of heart, to kneel before the Father."

The truth will set you free, and the truth is that God forgives you if you don't repeat the errors (and if you don't find enjoyment in lustful memories).

Let them go. Let guilt go. This will buffer you against attack.

Send up beams of light—not darkness.

When we don't forgive ourselves, it's a catch-22: we also find it hard to forgive others. And as a result, we may have stubborn "blocks" in our lives. We may subconsciously wish punishment (and even illness) upon ourselves. "Remember," said a hospice doctor, "forgiveness and love are positive attributes, so using them also summons the angels in large numbers. Just merely trying to change, forgive, and love will allow the angels to move toward healing and joy."

You can also design your own hell—here and perhaps hereafter. Don't let the judgments or jealousies of others keep you bound to past mistakes.

God is strict, yes. He has His rules. We obey them stringently. But when we have converted and confessed, we must move on.

He has washed us with His Blood.

What do you hold against yourself? What haven't you released? What sins still weigh on you?

Take them to the Cross.

"[A] reason why souls don't go to the Light is that they're afraid of being punished for what they did," wrote a woman who studied the afterlife. "And so the concourse between Heaven and earth is full of ghosts who have both minor infringements and great sins on their consciences. They don't believe that if only they could forgive themselves their sins, then God would forgive them too."

Give yourself a break. As the doctor noted, "it hurts God to think that one cannot find forgiveness, because He gave His only Son to the world. All we have to do is believe with all our hearts that His Son died for sins past, present, and future."

Scripture tells us that the truth liberates us and Jesus is the Truth and so if we have Him we should be free (*John* 8:32).

Too often, we're not. We're bound and wound and rewound with this world.

Tight like a watch—always watching time (which is one thing we're bound to).

There are many others. We're bound to people. Often, we cling to others in a way that's unhealthy (for them and us). We're bound to food. This is called gluttony. We're bound to technology—TV, computers, cell phones—which can be an addiction. We're bound to our thoughts. We're bound to our fears. We're bound to possessions (look at hoarders).

Are you bound to work? That means a workaholic. Are you bound to your home? Many won't wander far, due to fear—depriving themselves of experience (so tragic). We can also be bound to "good" things like exercise, if it becomes something very obsessive (throwing us out of balance; key word here, balance).

We need to let go. We restrict ourselves too much in life—out of insecurity. That's a lack of faith. What are you bound to? Where is your bondage? Is there something about which you obsess that causes you stress.

That's the marker. Stress. Eventually, it will break you.

It is ideal to adhere closely to every stricture and live by the spirit of those strictures but life is not cookie-cutter perfect and when we aren't flexible we are not free.

We can even be bound to our religion. A priest spoke of this the other day and gave the example of people who exhibit the "spirit of scrupulosity." If your husband or wife were ill and needed you at home, would you stay and miss Mass or chance it and leave him or her alone (for that hour or so) due to scrupulosity?

Do you follow the minutiae of the law at the expense of kindness?

If someone fell off a bridge, would you climb over a rail in an attempt to save him or not do so because it's technically against the law to climb over that railing?

It was the legalistic Pharisees and Sadducees who gave Jesus the most trouble and whom He most frequently admonished. (They attacked Him for healing on the Sabbath!) Religion is supposed to lead us to spirituality. "Let us tear their fetters apart and cast away their cords from us!" says *Psalm* 3:2.

Spirituality frees us.

When we are bound in fetters, says *Proverbs* (36:8), we're caught in the "cords of affliction."

Our religion is meant to lead to God and those who criticize others on legalistic grounds and who are themselves fastidious to the "t" in how they follow religion but are harsh and unloving must be careful. For it is this kind of zealotry that leads away from what Christ was really about (and may cause surprise in the afterlife).

The Lord wants to set us free but we're always building and rebuilding and structuring and creating our own creations and then clinging to the pillars and rules we have fashioned.

To a point, it is needed. We need laws. We need structure. We just also need to know that God wants us to flow with His Spirit. In not one single near-death episode does God conduct a life review in which He has a chalkboard with a long list of legal infractions.

Clinging is the operative word here. Do you cling? Do you inhibit family members or friends by clinging?

We cling to institutions. We cling to habits. We cling to old clothes. We cling to the world. We want everything structured because that makes us feel in control but when we look at how God moves we see the example of nature and wildlife where there is no stilted linear structure and yet where everything works together at the most complex levels in a way that's nothing less than astounding.

It is ideal to adhere closely to the law and live by the spirit of that law but when we aren't flexible we miss out on spontaneity and freedom.

Nature is free (as a bird).

Are we?

Do we "fly" with (and to) God?

Or are we earthbound?

"Shake yourself from the dust, rise up, O captive Jerusalem; Loose yourself from the chains around your neck, O captive daughter of Zion," says *Isaiah* 52:2.

Note how many times in your life that the best things you did or that happened to you were spontaneous—out of your routine.

In fact, when we break the strictness of a routine to do something for someone else we end up with more time to do what we were doing than we would have had otherwise.

God can even reshape time.

It is bondage that depresses us and causes insecurity and inhibits this great experience called life on earth (which is so very temporary—and exciting, when we let it be!).

41

Claim Your Blessings

There was once an eight-year-old boy who claimed to have "visited" Heaven and seen a place, there, of "unclaimed blessings."

Jesus showed him that in the realm of God are many benefits to help us on earth—gifts, emotions, healings—but said most go unclaimed because we don't ask for them!

Can you imagine that? *Unclaimed blessings.* Have you asked in faith for what *you* need? Have you been specific? Are you living life to the fullest—which means in deep prayer? Are you stepping with confidence—trust—or fear?

The boy, who later, as an adult, wrote a book called *We Saw Heaven*, said he even saw healthy organs for those who are sick and described the "place" of blessings as like store-houses that were almost full because so few take advantage of what they contain. "All you need to do is go in and get what you need by the hand of faith, because it is there!" he claimed. "You do not have to cry and beg God to make the part you need. Just go get it. The doors open for those who need to go in. We should empty those buildings!"

It is when we have fear that we block many blessings.

Fear is faith in a negative, allowing a negative to operate!

Often, we block blessings by not removing obstacles set in place by evil.

Satan causes many illnesses. Tear his grip away from you!

Go right for what is good.

Don't shy away.

Don't think you don't deserve it!

It's a matter of tenacity.

"Sometimes when we pray, an angel will leave Heaven to bring us the answer just as the angel did for Daniel, in *Daniel* 10:12, but will not be able to get through right away," says the boy in his book. "Daniel continued to pray and fast for twenty-one days until he received his answer. Because of his persistence in prayer, the angel was able to break through the demonic hindrances. What would have happened if Daniel had not kept praying and 'pressing on' to God for his answer?"

In another recent book (*Raising the Dead*) a cardiologist describes how a healer caused incredible effects by staring down evil and forcefully commanding it away instead of being afraid of it.

When the mother of another boy who was in a terrible accident (his spinal cord had been severed) arrived at the hospital, one of the paramedics was a faithful Christian who walked right over to her and boldly told her, "The Lord is already beginning the healing, but when you go in there, fear will try to attack your thinking. I'm not telling you to go in there and argue. Be polite and listen; they know what they're talking about. But as true as all their information is, God's Word can change all that. I prayed for your boy in the Name of Jesus, and he's not going to die. But if you go in there and agree with what they're saying and start speaking that, he will die. You'll negate what's been started by my praying for him. But if every time you get scared or hear a bad report, you thank the Lord for His healing, He will do His part. Have you got it?"

She did. The boy lived, despite what the doctors said.

Don't accept the evil report.

Doctors can be great and many are on an assignment from Heaven but there are those who operate solely through science and the ego of the intellectual and they can throw us curves; they can discourage; they can even hurt us. Look at how dangerous hospitals have become—because there is such a lack of prayer.

Don't fall victim. Seek correct medical attention but don't think for a moment that a doctor or surgeon has the last word.

No, that's God's domain. He can do anything; He can replace any part of our bodies. That boy with the severed spine? He lived! The newspapers called it a "miracle."

There are hundreds of similar accounts.

God wants you well. There are challenges. But more in number are the blessings.

Go and claim what is yours. Claim wellness. Claim a cure. Claim the end of financial distress. Claim removal of the devil. The Lord wraps them all the time—gift-wraps them, with the ribbon of the Cross—and sighs when they go unopened.

Don't let your internal "baggage" prevent a blessing.

Aggravations? Hurts? A hurtful memory? A dispute?

Let them pass and they will pass. Learn to pray more "for" something than against something. Pray and receive more. As for negativity: let it go and you will grow. They are lessons for us as we approach life with the strength of "manger faith." Take no offense when you are turned away from the inn. Forge ahead.

All clouds—however dark—dissipate with time, unless we feed them the moisture of wrong emotion.

Let go of lusts. Often, lust is the blockage (and causes a blockage in your heart). If you have trouble loving or praying from the heart, lust could be the "log."

Let go of phobias, wrong attitudes, habits, routine, grudges, inferiority, fear of failure, wrong friendships . . . Make a list.

Again, let go of your guilt:

Let's listen to a deliverance expert named Don Dickerman, who in a new book called *Keep the Pigs Out* said: "After a believer has become free from demonic intrusion, one of the giant doorways for demons to gain a new entry point is revisiting the past. It's like probing a wound that is almost healed. It's re-aggravating a nagging injury so that it cannot heal. When you relive a past failure or an unpleasant time in your life, you are allowing demons another opportunity to use the incident once more against you. Don't go there. You must control that part of your thinking, or the demons will. You can choose to not think about the past, and when you do this, you seize any opportunities that demons may have had to torment you. Remember that fret and regret are two bad dogs; don't let them in. You must take those thoughts captive! By faith, apply the Blood of Jesus to the part of your mind that seems to be in replay mode. Speak your choice to dwell on pleasant and hopeful thoughts."

When Jesus delivered people from demonic infestation, His ejection of unclean spirits was final. He sealed the soul against re-entry.

Seal yours.

Let go of the mistakes of your youth; let go of those memories of a relationship that went awry, or never should have been. Confess, repent, and move on. Let go of the insults that still plague you.

Fly above the problem and you'll fly *under* the devil's radar.

Staring up at a cloud only gets rain on you.

Said Dickerman: "One of the things we see healed on a regular basis when this is done is fibromyalgia. If pleasant words and a cheerful heart are health to the bones, what is anger and bitterness to the bones? If repentance and departing from evil is health and marrow to the bones, what is holding on to unforgiveness?"

The same goes for sin.

"Father," we can say, *"I confess of the sin of sexual relations outside of marriage, or wrong relations even within, and I renounce that sinful activity in Jesus' Name. I call back that part of me that was given to another, and I refuse that part of another that may have come to me. I denounce soul ties with [say name] and choose to be free in the Name of Jesus Christ. Amen!"*

Do this with your list and you will feel it lift. Give it to yourself as a gift for your birthday, for Christmas. Fill your stockings with *right thinking* and that faith of the manger. "Lord, give me a new and right spirit. Cleanse my soul. Cleanse my thoughts. Cleanse my motive. Cleanse what I like. Cleanse what I do. Cleanse what I say. Cleanse who I am."

"God will not cover our sin until we uncover it to Him," noted Dickerman. "As long as we keep it hidden, it remains exposed to demons who seize upon the legal right of unconfessed sin."

What you expect is what you will project on the reality of your future. It is in the inner recesses of the mind that we build or reinforce or lessen or destroy blessings that God has for us.

The Lord is always the One Who determines what occurs—it's not like we can program every single thing by positive thinking (see *Job*)—nor does He grant us every material whim (especially not selfish ones). But most often a "right expectation" (purity of intention) propels us to success in work, health, and matters that are important to us. Right expectation is expecting the best and takes practice and *rhythm*. It's more powerful than you think.

Notice how rhythm works. It has to do with correct habits. First, we have to break the inertia of doing the wrong thing or doing nothing at all and then form the right way into a routine. We have to become accustomed to something new. We have to carve a new groove. We see this especially with work and exercise. It's only a big deal when we sit around thinking about (or dreading) it.

Once you simply get up and *do* it and cut a groove it flows smoothly.

Let your groove be right thinking. Once you start, you gain momentum. Expect the best. Expect more. Work with diligence. Pray at every chance. Get into the habit of dressing neatly. Rest when you need it. Especially, get into the rhythm of cleansing your thought process. (This is the attire of your spirit.)

Adopt the habit of casting out your own darkness before noting the darkness in others.

Darkness is sin. Darkness is a bad habit. Darkness is pride. Darkness is anger. Darkness is lust. Darkness is antagonism. Darkness is bias. Darkness is sloppiness. Darkness is distortion. Darkness is hate. Darkness is materialism. Darkness is laziness (sloth). Darkness is the wrong rhythm. We sin more than we realize!

Get in the daily rhythm of reading Scripture.

"The Lord answered Job out of the storm and said, 'Now gird up your loins like a man; I will ask you, and you instruct Me. Will you really annul My judgment? Will you

Michael Harold Brown

condemn Me that you may be justified? Or do you have an arm like God, and can you thunder with a voice like His? Adorn yourself with eminence and dignity, and clothe yourself with honor and majesty. Pour out the overflowings of your anger'" (*Job* 40:7-11).

Just recently, the Pope referred back to the Roman Empire and how as it fell due to impurity it was plagued by natural disasters as we see disasters unnerving us in our current time. That's because we are in the rhythm of selfishness. *Me, me, me.* Worldliness is darkness and we could define it as politics, money, and entertainment, when it's not used for the glory of God. It's the wrong rhythm to follow. How many of us do? How many of us have one foot in Christianity and the other in worldliness? The rhythm of right living is His Glory and only His. This means *purity of intention*. Do it for Him. There is no better rhythm! Without pure intentions we are expecting a blessing the wrong way (and thus prayer is often unanswered).

Darkness also comes from others:

When we allow people to define us, it distorts who we think we are and throws us off course. It breaks our pace. It brings the wrong expectation. This occurs when we cowtow to the misguided notions of relatives or friends or those with whom we work or when we allow others to cause us to view ourselves in a way that is negative because they are judging by the standards of the world.

People pile things onto us or we do it to ourselves and when our perspective is distorted we wander from the path set for us. It brings the wrong expectation.

Free yourself. Cleanse yourself. Did you know that the elevated Host breaks bonds? Did you know you can "bathe" yourself (wash yourself of the cardinal sins) with the Rosary (and of course Confession)? "From my secret sins cleanse, me, oh Lord."

220

Take a deep breath and exhale darkness.

Seal yourself with the Holy Spirit.

Breathe in the living waters. Ask the Lord to make your heart as white as the Host.

Surround yourself with angels. "The hope of the righteous is gladness," (*Proverbs* 10:28).

The great mission of life is to purify and right our spirits as we accomplish the tasks set forth in the course of our lives and it does little good to live a long life unless we are in a constant rhythm of purification!

Get back to the rhythm of God. Get back to who you really are. Flow with the rhythm of who God made you to be; you'll find it at Mass; you'll find the pace in deep prayer. You'll find it fasting. Give prayer a chance. Don't rush. (That's the wrong rhythm.) Expect God to repair past damage (as He did for Job, who, in the end, expected it).

God created everything. All is under His domain. And it is a great test of life to see if we can abandon our troubles and sufferings and ourselves to Him as did Jesus at Calvary.

When we do, we open the way for potential miracles. We can move the "mountain." The Lord breathes our way. We ascend. Perhaps better put: His power intensifies around us.

The Blessed Mother has said that with enough prayer, we will not even feel the passage into the eternal. Magnify the Lord, not illness, not hardship, not fear, not brokenness. Lord, I love You. My God, You are my Everything. To You and You only are my eyes fixed—oh Great One, Lord of Lords, praise You, Creator not just of earth but of the cosmos, and eternities beyond.

42

Your Blessings are Where Things Fall Into Place

God has a plan for you and you find it in what occurs around you. He has a *destiny* for you. It's in everything that has happened to you—and that you are blessed with.

There's a set course for your life and it may shift according to the actions of our free will but that destiny remains in its essence and is meant to play out when our time on earth comes to an end.

There's a plan for you and the paths are shown in both the problems you face and the blessings.

Sit down and reflect in prayer on the major intersections of your life.

Map them out. Note the way events occurred when you were on the wrong course and when you were on the right one; look how events interwove!

Blessings direct our paths. Do we take them for granted—or use them to map our lives?

You were given certain talents. Everyone has talents. It could be as a housewife. It could be as an engineer. It could be as a janitor.

You were given parents. How have they affected you? What would your life be without their guidance? How often do you consider them a gift? Many have been given husbands and wives. How often do we wonder at the circumstances of our marriages—and how important we are to each other, in God's scheme? How has marriage affected the course of your life—and the way you developed spiritually? What guideposts and challenges came with matrimony—and what they tell you about yourself? A meditation this is! Likewise, how often do we mull over the gift of our children? How have *they* affected us? Why were they placed with us? And how does a family move together toward God's Plan?

Do we consider a blessing as just something that has occurred—"good luck"—or treat each as a guidepost? How often do we study the circumstances in our lives and the way one thing led to another—right under our noses but without our notice because we were swept into "normal" thinking?

"At the moment of my death I awoke from a darkness," recounted a young German woman named Ann whose account of an incredible dream was authorized by her diocese years ago. "I found myself suddenly enveloped by a blinding light. It was at the same place where my body lay. It seemed almost like a theater, when the lights suddenly go out, the curtain noisily opens, and a tragically illuminated scene appears: the scene of my life. I saw my soul as in a mirror.

"I saw the graces I had trampled underfoot since the time I was young."

Too often, we take the blessing of a job as just a job. We take the blessing of a loaf of bread as just a loaf of bread. We take the blessing of a house as just a house. But look at the fortuitous events God orchestrated in order for us to have that security.

It is when you fully acknowledge and *know* a blessing that other blessings will come.

Look more closely at how certain events fell into place.

Work the puzzle.

Study your life and note the dovetails.

When we take blessings for granted, we take God for granted. Big mistake!

In the blessings—as in troubles—are those life missions.

You will see your path.

It is defined by what we are given and what is taken away and the challenges and crises.

Don't aim for excitement when you should be aiming for joy. Do you choose thrills over happiness? Do you prefer what's loud over what is quiet? Have you ever thought of the difference?

From time to time, most of us prefer quick excitement; too often. We look for what *titillates*. We look for that rush of adrenalin. It even becomes our goal. We go for what is a flash in the pan—*what is sudden and intense and fleeting* (quicksilver)—instead of happiness—joy—that's lasting.

Like quicksilver (the substance at the back of a mirror), it is backwards; it can be a self-centered illusion. Don't confuse excitement with contentment.

There are good excitements; it is great, perhaps, for the right reason, to be thrilled; but overall we should not be thrill-seeking. We should avoid frenzy. We should avoid screaming and cheering that becomes raucous.

Joy is what brings contentment (and health) to the soul!

And often it is to be found in what is quiet.

The antidote to the rush of modern adrenalin and the carnality of life is in what is wordless.

"Silence is a sword in the spiritual struggle," wrote Saint Faustina Kowalska of Divine Mercy renown. "A talkative soul will never attain sanctity. The sword of silence will cut off everything that would like to cling to the soul. We are sensitive to words and quickly want to answer back, without taking any regard as to whether it is God's Will that we should speak. A silent soul is strong. No adversities will harm it if it perseveres in silence. The silent soul is capable of attaining the closest union with God. It lives almost always under the inspiration of the Holy Spirit. God works in a silent soul without hindrance."

Have you ever meditated on the power of silence—especially when so much news whirls around us? Have you ever looked back on your life and noticed the way a crisis or conflict may have been averted by practicing reserve? Have you ever "fasted" from impulsiveness (and seen the fruits)?

Quick triggers shoot randomly and miss their targets.

Meditate as did St. Faustina when she wrote:

"Oh day most solemn, oh day of brightness, when the soul will know God in His omnipotence and drown totally in His Love, knowing the miseries of exile are o'er.

"Oh happy day, oh blessed day, when my heart will burn for You with fire eternal. For even now I feel Your Presence, though through the veil.

"Through life and death, oh Jesus, You are my rapture and my delight.

"Oh day, of which I dreamed through all my life, for it is You alone Whom I desire. You are the One and only of my heart; all else is naught.

"Oh day of delight, day of eternal bliss, God of great majesty, my beloved Spouse, You know that nothing will satisfy a virgin heart. On Your tender Heart I rest my brow."

Ungratefulness and pride build walls that separate us from God while humility is the bridge to Heaven.

God illuminates with shafts of pure anointing and tapping into that brilliance is the key to the miraculous. That is an important message for our time: We live at a moment in history when science is trying to declaim anything that may be a wonder, and when even many in religious institutions have lost belief in such interventions.

It is important to constantly invoke the Holy Spirit in the Name of Jesus.

Prayer affords the opportunity for the Holy Spirit to work within us—and He does so in many ways that are without explanation. Time and again I have seen miracles spring from faith if that faith is unwavering.

Only with humility do we receive gifts. If we are full of pride, there is no room. Gifts bounce off of us. It is like oil. It is unction. It doesn't go with the Living Waters. On the other hand, humility attracts goodness. God resists the proud.

Pride and lack of love hold us back more than anything else from the joy of direct entry into Heaven (and blessings here).

Seek that direct entry.

You can do it.

Your life is a role on stage and you will see it all replayed in your life review.

So treat each and every action in life as if you will see it again (for you will).

Consider everyone equal. Don't contort your self perspective. Contemplate your self-perception. Seek balance. The ego makes you see yourself as in a carnival mirror (either too big or too small; disjointed).

When you look in the mirror, see a servant.

What about the "Job experience"? You hurt your back. You develop allergies. You have a serious skin disorder. You have aching joints. You suddenly have fibromyalgia. You have an accident. The roof leaks. You lose a loved one.

Finances collapse. For some folks, serious illnesses like cancer and heart disease are thrown into the mix. Never mind a leak; the roof seems to cave in. One sickness, one setback, one disappointment, one suffering after another. This can come for a number of reasons. It can come because we are neglecting something in our spiritual or temporal lives. It can occur simply in the course of the life's trials. It can occur due to a hidden block (or curse). It can happen due to sin. It can be something that has been passed down through the generations. "I cry to Thee and Thou dost not heed me," Job bellowed.

Don't come under the power of a curse.

Also, bless yourself:

I can do that. I will make it. I will fulfill my destiny.

While only priests grant special blessings (for example, at the end of Mass, and when they bless sacramentals), everyone is allowed—and called—to bless each other on a regular basis.

We bless meals before we eat. We bless each other when we sneeze. We say "God bless you" as a matter of daily talk (or should). We ask for blessings in the confessional.

What about blessings of deliverance?

If we do this effectively, our dear ones then pass these blessings on to their children, and their children to *their* offspring—down the generations.

In Scripture, there was special power attached to a father's blessing. Blessings were an integral part of God's relationship with Abraham (*Genesis* 12:1, 2, 3). And look at his descendants, such as Isaac: When he blessed his son Jacob (*Genesis* 27:30) it was a blessing that caused livestock to thrive under his care and brought him success for many years in all aspects of life (a blessing that lasted).

There is what they call the "Aaronic blessing." This comes from *Numbers* 6:23-27—and it has special power.

Listen closely. It came when the Lord spoke to Moses and said, "Speak to Aaron and to his sons, saying, 'Thus you shall bless the sons of Israel. You shall say to them:

"'*The Lord bless you, and keep you; the Lord make His Face shine upon you, and be gracious to you; the Lord lift up His countenance to you.'*"

(Said God: "So shall they invoke My Name on the sons of Israel, and I then will bless them.")

Write it down. Pass it on. Give the special Old Testament blessing to your spouse and children: "*The Lord bless you, and keep you; the Lord make His Face shine upon you, and be gracious to you; the Lord lift up His countenance to you.*" Husbands, use it regularly on your wives; wives, use it on your husbands; parents, use it on your children (and children, on your parents!) It seals against evil. Release the blessing of God as did the anointed ones of Israel. We can add: say it in the Name of the Infant Jesus.

Use it also to bless those who "curse" you! Many report miracles with it. Through such prayer, a curse is turned into a blessing.

One preacher who uses it described a woman from India whose mother wanted a son and had cursed her during childhood. The girl resented her mom and as a result, developed a strange large, V-shaped "birthmark" on her forehead. She was told to send her mother a blessing—instead of resenting her—and when she did, the mark faded, even disappeared. (When the resentment returned, so did the birthmark—until she forgave and blessed again!)

There are many ways of declaring a blessing.

In prayer—out loud—declare your home a zone of health.

Declare it a "cancer-free zone."

Declare it a zone of love.

"*The Lord bless you, and keep you; the Lord make His Face shine upon you, and be gracious to you; the Lord lift up His countenance to you.*"

This is healing. There are special blessings. Gather together those you love and light a holy candle (or use Holy Water) and pray the blessing upon everyone.

I had a word of knowledge one Christmas night:

"*I bless those who bless others; I anoint those who use their anointing to help others. I send grace through those who let My Graces flow through them, as does the Blessed Mother, in health and Heaven.*"

43

Purity for All of Infinity

The goal in life should be to cleanse all that spiritual grit by the time we die and that is done by looking toward the Eucharist as both a cleansing agent and an example.

Through Communion we can present our inner darkness to the Lord and fill ourselves with Him.

Whiten your soul to the color of the Eucharist.

Heaven is that level of white and we can step into it only if our own whiteness matches it.

Clarity in full; purity in all infinity:

The goal of life should be to die in a state of innocence—in the squeaky cleanliness of our "first creation."

Those are potent words. It means how we were born into this world.

If we can achieve that—if we can re-establish such innocence—we achieve the ultimate blessing: Heaven.

Purity. Openness. Innocence. Think about it:

Ever since birth, we've fought off the grit of temptation. The devil has tried to soil that garb we will bring to eternity. As we grow in our Christianity, Christ prunes dark spots. "If necessary, He will risk your misunderstanding of His methods and motives," writes another, Bruce Wilkinson. "His purpose is for you to cut away immature commitments and lesser priorities to make room for even greater abundance for His glory." In pruning, how we respond makes all the difference. When we suffer, notes this author, we should offer it up to Jesus and respond with joy, comfort, and gratitude—not complaint or rebellion.

Think about it: once you came to Jesus, did you notice how certain of your relationships changed, and how hanging out with certain friends began making you feel empty or out of place? Indeed, we start to gravitate to people who are on the devout side. They're the ones that now fulfill us.

This isn't to exclude people, and this isn't to encourage folks to ditch long friendships (and certainly not spouses!). It's to advise us that we must go with the flow of the Lord—and recognize when God is weaning us.

He weans us from money, physical attachments, and bad habits. His first command is to seek first the Kingdom of God, and as Wilkinson points out, "this is why God will always prune those things that we slavishly seek first, love most, and begrudge giving up. Again, His goal isn't to plunder or harm, but to liberate us so that we can pursue our true desire—His Kingdom."

If disciplining is about sinfulness, weaning is about ego. The Lord wants us to let go of things that inhibit us; He wants us to ditch what is unnecessary; He wants what's best for our ultimate good. It's how the Lord changes us from an empty basket to one full of fruit!

And if you really want to bear fruit, try this little prayer each day: "Lord, let me make a difference for You that is utterly disproportionate to who I am."

The more we appreciate the interchange between the physical and spiritual, the more we flow in the stream of life, which means gaining momentum toward larger miracles. Building faith means watching little prayers build into bigger ones.

How good is God! How miraculous! That He would even create us! When we see the constant miracles of life, we begin to view everything from a spiritual perspective.

The key to gaining Heaven is to live every moment in the way we would want to be judged. The key is to live each moment as if it is our last. Our hearts must be filled with gladness, which is a miracle, a gift like every gift that flows from the Holy Spirit. It is available to everyone and joins the important component of hope, which means to look at all matters from a positive aspect: not a Pollyanna aspect, where we try to make it seem like even something truly bad is good, but rather a knowing that there is a light at the end of the tunnel—literally.

Often we miss out on a miracle because we gave up or simply didn't pray enough.

Once I spotted a severe thunderstorm coming. It had not been predicted by the weatherman, yet it looked very intense, the most swiftly-moving, blackest clouds I'd ever seen. It was a localized storm, heading directly our way, and it was hurling tremendous bolts of lightning.

Immediately I asked God to keep the lightning off our property and it was a very specific request: that it not hit our house. Quickly, I made the Sign of the Cross to "cover" our lot.

The storm struck and lightning hit, all right—missing our house, hitting just feet from our back property line.

That was an answer to a prayer—and a specific answer at that. It missed our yard! But the story doesn't end there. There was a surge of electricity that swept underground, carrying into the power, cable, and telephone lines, which caused problems in our home.

Our burglar alarm had to be replaced. Two outlets were burned out. A computer was damaged.

And in my mind the reason was simple: I had not perse-vered. I had not prayed long or thoroughly enough. I had uttered the quick prayer of protection over our property and that had worked, but I had not prayed to protect us from any surge, had not prayed to protect specific items like our computers, alarm system, and other equipment, and had not prayed for the neighborhood in general.

There was a miracle in how the storm had missed us but the miracle could have been bigger. With more prayer, we would not have lost any equipment.

Complete prayer brings larger results.

Why do storms serve as such a good example?

It was during a storm that Jesus admonished His disci-ples to step out of the boat and into the realm of miracles.

God is love. Love is light. Light is life. God is the Light of life that loves. What heals is love; what kills is judgment. The Light itself is only love. Of all the teachings, the greatest is love. It is accompanied by joy, which is the truest sign that we are living right. Joy in all, joy in Jesus.

"Whenever a person turns to the Lord the veil is removed," says *2 Corinthians* 3:15. "Now the Lord is the Spirit and where the Spirit of the Lord is, there is freedom. All of us, gazing with unveiled face on the glory of the Lord, are being transformed into the same image from glory to glory, as from the Lord Who is the Spirit."

Life is a test full of thorns and trials and once we realize that, we transcend it.

God has blessings for you, blessings you don't even know are there, blessings you may not even have requested. Our Lord is a giving God and He has all *kinds* of blessings in store for you. He has happiness. He has contentment. He has security.

Those are gifts He may have wrapped for you and it may be time to claim them. I'm not talking about material things (although they may figure into it). I'm talking about grace.

The Lord has abundant graces assigned to each of you, and when you get to Heaven, you'll see the extent of them. He may be ready to give you gifts of joy, patience, prayer, love, friends, insights, peace, and well-being. There's no telling *what* he has wrapped for you, and the point is to realize them now—to claim them—so there won't be regrets later, in the afterlife, when you'll be able to see the entire plan for your life.

What a promise this is! The Lord wants you to live life to the fullest and if you follow His precepts—clearly marked out in the New Testament—you will find what you have yearned for (albeit not always in the way you have yearned for it). The Lord wants us to have life and life abundantly and He wants us to live in the joy of knowing that earth is but a trial and that beyond that is His Kingdom.

He grants blessings in the same way that there are holiday gifts. Often He grants us what we request, but just as often He catches us off-guard. Often, He gives us things we *didn't* ask for. He surprises. There are big gifts. There are small gifts. There are gifts that seem minor until we mature enough to appreciate them. Suddenly we turn a corner, and there it is: something from the Lord that sets us right and changes us in a way that's like manna from the sky and makes life all the better.

That's how generous God is. He's always looking to make us happy, but like any parent He doesn't give us things that are not good for us. When we die, we'll see the many things we sought that would have caused us damage. It will be remarkable to see God's plan for our lives laid out in ways we couldn't grasp while we were wearing blinders.

There's no telling what He has in store for you. It could be a spouse, it could be a new job, it could be solving a problem with a son or daughter or friend. It could be the opportunity of suffering.

He does this with us all. He sheds grace when we least expect it. When we're faithful and don't complain and don't try to tell God the way everything in our lives should go, He responds with a flurry of the (good) unexpected.

The key word is "release": Release your desires to the Lord. Release all that is causing you anxiety. In prayer, go through all that may be causing you angst. Hand it over to Christ. Release your desire. Release all your fears. This is very powerful in communicating with the Almighty One. Invite God to surprise you every day and no day will bore you!

And remember the Blessed Mother:

"O Mary, my mother and Our Lady of Surprises, what a happy joy you caused the wedding guests, when you asked your Divine Son to work the miracle of water into wine. What a happy surprise for them since they thought the wine had run dry. I, too, Mary, love surprises and as your child, may I ask you to favor me with one today? I ask this only because you are my ever caring mother."

You may be amazed at what she brings you.

Be holy. Know that there are blessings around the corner. Be personal with Jesus.

That combination will loose blessings and lift you in a way that will exceed even your favorite Christmas.

Many who come back from "death" recount what one witness described as "this pure crystal clear light, an illuminating white light. It was beautiful and so bright, so radiant, but it didn't hurt my eyes. It's not like any kind of light you can describe on earth."

This is the light that clothes us when we reach the right level of purity. This is the light we can begin to surround ourselves with here on earth. "I became fascinated by the fabric of his robe, trying to figure out how light could be woven!" said another.

"At the end of the table closest to me was a man sitting in a throne type chair; He was clothed in a white robe," said a woman describing Jesus.

"Immediately after leaving my body a shaft of very white light came down in the room and a beautiful woman with long black hair in a white robe trimmed in gold came down through the Light," is a third testimony. "She extended her hands toward me and gave me the choice of either going up in the Light with her or staying on earth in my body. At first, I wanted to go with her in the Light as the experience was so beautiful and peaceful. I was also totally out of pain as the Light surrounded me."

"I had no body but I could see a man dressed in a brilliant white robe," says *yet* another. "His clothes were as bright as a lightning bolt."

"I noted that all four of us were wearing traditional flowing white robes (traditional in the sense of what you might have seen people wearing around the first century, not the flimsy, silky type of robe we often see Jesus depicted in), although mine was slightly whiter or brighter than those of the angels around me," said an minister who died named Lonnie Honeycutt.

And we hear:

"There was a brilliant, brilliant light all around us—all around me and everything else. In fact, the word I choose to use to describe my entire time in Heaven is 'brilliant.'"

"Blessed are those who wash their robes," says *Revelation* 22:14, "so that they may have the right to the tree of life, and may enter by the gates into the city."

Go back. Pray about every year in your life. Replace darkness with light. Take Communion for this cause—repeatedly. Let not a patch of unforgiveness, or lust, or falsity, or vengefulness, or jealousy, or resentment, or anger, or addiction, or greed, or selfishness cause a blot on what you will one day wear. You don't want to wear your bad habits! (Everyone sees every truth in Heaven.)

Prepare now and step into the immaculate and brilliant state we are called to emulate by the Immaculate Virgin Mary.

And remember always: what kills is judgment; what heals is love.

Appendix

Forgiveness Prayer

Lord Jesus Christ, I ask today to forgive everyone in my life. I know that You will give me strength to forgive and I thank You that You love me more than I love myself and want my happiness more than I desire it for myself.

Lord Jesus, I want to be free from the feelings of resentment, bitterness, and unforgiveness toward You for the times I thought You sent death, hardships, financial difficulties, punishments and sickness into our family.

Lord, I forgive myself for my sins, faults and failings. For all that is truly bad in myself or all that I think is bad, I do forgive myself. For any delvings in the occult: Ouija boards, horoscopes, seances, fortune telling, lucky charms, for taking Your name in vain, for not worshiping You, for hurting my parents, for getting drunk, for taking dope, for sins against my purity, for adultery, for abortion, for stealing, for lying. I am truly forgiving myself today. Thank you, Lord, for Your grace at this moment.

I truly forgive my mother. I forgive her for all the times she hurt me, resented me, was angry with me and for all the times she punished me. I forgive her for the times she preferred my brothers and sisters to me. I forgive her for the times she told me I was dumb, ugly, stupid, the worst of the children or that I cost the family a lot of money. For the times she told me I was unwanted, an accident, a mistake or not what she expected, I forgive her.

I forgive my father. I forgive him for any nonsupport, any lack of love, affection or attention. I forgive him for any lack of time, for not giving me his companionship, for his drinking or arguing and fighting with my mother or the other children. For his severe punishments, for desertion, for being away from home, for divorcing my mother or for any running around, I do forgive him.

Lord, I extend forgiveness to my sisters and brothers. I forgive those who rejected me, lied about me, hated me, resented me, and competed for my parents' love, those who hurt me, who physically harmed me. For those who were too severe on me, punished me or made my life unpleasant in any way, I do forgive them.

Lord, I forgive my spouse for lack of love, affection, consideration, support, attention, communications, for faults, failings, weaknesses and those other acts or words that hurt or disturb me.

Jesus, I forgive my children for their lack of respect, obedience, love, attention, support, warmth, understanding, their bad habits, falling away from the church and bad actions which disturb me.

My God, I forgive my in-laws, mother, father, son or daughter-in-law and other relatives by marriage. For their lack of love, words of criticism, thoughts, actions or omissions that injure and cause pain, I do forgive them.

Please help me to forgive my relatives, my grandmother and grandfather who may have interfered in our family, been possessive of my parents, who may have caused confusion or turned one parent against the other.

Jesus, help me to forgive my co-workers who are disagreeable or make life miserable for me. For those who push their work off on me, gossip about me, won't cooperate with me, try to take my job, I do forgive them.

My neighbors need to be forgiven, Lord. For all their noise, letting their property run down, not tying up their dogs who run through my yard, not taking in their trashcans, being prejudiced and running down the neighborhood, I do forgive them.

I now forgive my clergyman, my congregation and my church for all their lack of support, pettiness, bad sermons, lack of friendliness, not affirming me as they should, not providing me with inspiration, for not using me in a key position, for not inviting me to serve in a major capacity and for any other hurt they have inflicted. I do forgive them today.

Lord, I forgive all professional people who have hurt me in any way: doctors, lawyers, policemen, hospital workers, for the things that they did to me, I truly forgive them today.

Lord, I forgive my employer for not paying me enough money, for not appreciating my work, for being unkind and unreasonable with me, for being angry or unfriendly, for not promoting me and for not complimenting me on my work.

Lord, I forgive my schoolteachers and instructors of the past, as well as the present. For those who punished me, humiliated me, insulted me, treated me unjustly, made fun of me, called me dumb or stupid, made me stay after school.

Lord, I forgive my friends who have let me down, lost contact with me, do not support me, were not available when I needed help, borrowed money and did not return it, gossiped about me.

Lord Jesus, I especially pray for the grace of forgiveness for that one person in life who has hurt me the most. I ask to forgive anyone who I consider my greatest enemy; the one who is the hardest to forgive or the one who I said I would never forgive.

Thank You, Jesus, that I am free of the evil of unforgiveness. Let Your Holy Spirit fill me with light and let every dark area of my mind be enlightened.

Amen.

Notes and Acknowledgements

I would like to thank my wife, Lisa, as always, for her excellent counsel and editing and encouragement and love! My thanks to Judy Berlinski for editing and formatting so finely, and to Peter Massari for his cover – splendid as usual. Thanks to my sister Kathleen Jenkins for proof-reading. And to all who have sent me their accounts and who read our website, www.spiritdaily.com.